LIVING AND LEADING WELL:

Navigating Mid-Life Ministry

By

DR. RICHARD CLINTON AND
PAUL LEAVENWORTH

ISBN: 1481230638

ISBN 13: 9781481230636

Library of Congress Control Number: XXXXX

LCCN Imprint Name: City and State

Table of Contents

About the Authors

Richard Clinton is currently the Senior Pastor of a Vineyard Church in Colorado Springs, CO. Before taking his current position he served in pastoral roles at other Vineyards in the U.S. and Switzerland. He has also served as an Adjunct Assistant Professor of Leadership at Fuller Theological Seminary (CA) and as the Director of Barnabas Resources, an organization committed to "equipping, training, and releasing effective leaders into service for the Kingdom of God."

Richard completed his undergraduate studies at Westmont College (CA) and his M.A., M.Div., and D.Min. at Fuller Theological Seminary. His father, Dr. J. Robert (Bobby) Clinton has recently retired after forty plus years as a Professor of Leadership in the School of Intercultural Studies at Fuller Seminary.

Over the past several years Richard and Bobby have co-ministered together in the area of leadership training and development while developing the Clinton Leadership Institute (www.jrclintoninstitute.com) to continue the process of Biblical research in leadership development.

Richard is married and has three sons. He currently lives in Monument, CO.

Paul Leavenworth is currently the Executive Director for the Convergence group (www.theconvergencegroup.org), a consulting organization committed to helping leaders finish well. Before taking his current position he served as the Executive Director for Leadership Development and Church Ministries for Open Bible Churches. He has also served as an instructor at Eugene Bible College (now New Hope Christian College), a missionary with YWAM, and a college administrator at Christian liberal arts colleges.

He completed his undergraduate studies at Oregon State University and has completed an M.A. in Theology at Fuller Theological Seminary. He has also completed a M.Ed. in Guidance and Counseling from Whitworth College (WA) and an Ed.D. in Counseling from the College of William and Mary (VA).

Paul is married and has three children and currently lives in West Des Moines, IA.

Preface

It is hard to believe that almost twenty years ago Richard Clinton and I (Paul Leavenworth) wrote *Starting Well: Building a Strong Foundation for a Lifetime of Ministry*. Our hope back in 1994 was to get an established publishing company to edit and publish our work. We felt that there was a need for Biblically based materials designed to help young emerging leaders establish a foundation of intimacy with God and integrity in life and ministry.

I still remember getting the rejection letters back from publishers. The letters went something like this,

> "Good content... needs editing... we do not think there is a market for a book like this... Thanks, but no thanks!"

Richard and I were disappointed but convinced that there was a need (even if there was not a market) for a book like *Starting Well*. Both of us were in teaching situations at the time so we made copies of our rough draft and used the materials in our classes.

Fortunately, Richard's father, J. Robert Clinton, Professor of Leadership (now retired) at Fuller Seminary in Pasadena, CA, had established Barnabas Publishers (in his garage) to publish his research on Biblically based leadership development and offered to publish a thousand copies of *Starting Well* through Barnabas.

Little did we know at the time that over the years *Starting Well* would be translated in Spanish, German, Korean, and Indonesian and become a textbook in Bible colleges, seminaries, and other youth training programs (YWAM, Master's Commissions, etc.).

When Richard and I wrote *Starting Well*, I had a sense that we would be co-authoring two sequels, *Living and Leading Well* and *Finishing Well*, at some time in the future. We have waited for several years to write *Living and Leading Well* because we wanted to be able to write from experience not just theory.

The events surrounding the resignation and firing of a prominent Evangelical leader in late 2008 was a wake up call for many of us. Although I did not know this person personally, my boss at the time knew him and was on his executive board. I had read several of his books and heard him speak at a couple of conferences.

I had great respect for him and his ministry and was shocked when I heard of his "fall." He seemed to be doing so many things in ministry well and I was especially encouraged by his commitment to developing young emerging leaders. If he could fall, then it could happen to anybody.

One does not have to think very hard to come up with multiple other examples of once prominent, powerful, and influential people who have fallen - whether it is in the realm of politics, business, education, entertainment, sports, etc. Just because a person looks good on the outside (at least for awhile), does not mean that they are all together on the inside. Time and life's pressures have a way of exposing who we really are.

I am reminded of a couple of weighty passages in the Bible that talk about this dynamic. The first is I Peter 5: 4 which says, "God opposes the proud, but gives grace to the humble" (NIV). This is a direct quote from the Old Testament Proverbs (3: 34) and is the basis for Peter's teaching that humility is the kingdom way of effective life and leadership.

The other passage that comes to mind is found in Galatians 6: 7. It says, "Do not be deceived: God cannot be mocked. A man reaps what he sows" (NIV). Life and its many challenges will eventually expose us for who we really are!

Pretty heavy stuff! This should cause us to gain a more mature understanding of the fear of God. We are weak and vulnerable in our humanity. As a faithful friend and mentor reminds me regularly, "We are just one banana peel away from a pretty major fall!"

Our Vision

Our vision in writing *Living and Leading Well* is to provide Biblically based insights, strategies, and resources to help mid-life "ministers" (whether they minister in the context of the church, marketplace, or other social settings) navigate the challenges that come with getting older, raising kids, and adjusting goals to the realities of mid-life.

We have co-authored this book because Richard and I are in the midst of learning how to navigate mid-life and we each bring unique life experience, ministry experience, and gifting to this project. We also believe that there is "synergy" in collaboration. Bobby Clinton has mentored both Richard and me in his leadership development paradigm and each of us is attempting to apply his research findings in our own settings. Richard is navigating mid-life as a pastor of a local church. I am navigating the later stages of mid-life as I enter into semi-retirement in my early "senior" years as a consultant and coach helping leaders finish well.

We trust that through our collaboration there will be a greater perspective on critical mid-life issues that will connect with a greater spectrum of types of people. Each of us has authored individual chapters based on our interests, expertise, and life experiences.

Our Goals

This project is designed to integrate Biblical leadership principles, lessons, and examples with real life experiences to help the reader to understand the dynamics and challenges of mid-life in order to navigate them in such a way that they do not hinder God's ultimate purposes for their lives. To put it simply, our goal is to help mid-life men and women who have started well and want to finish well, to live and lead well!

Richard and I write from a two-fold bias: 1. A Male perspective, for obvious reasons, and 2. A Ministry perspective, because that is where we have primarily served. We do believe that the following material is applicable for men and women who serve in ministry and the marketplace, although you may have to get acquainted with our language and translate it for your own understanding.

With this in mind, we believe that there are Biblical principles that can be understood and applied that will help us to start, live and lead, and finish well. Our focus in this book is on living and leading well. The goals of this project include:

1. **Providing an overview of the leadership "landscape" of mid-life so that we can anticipate challenges and opportunities in order to cooperate with God in his purposes.**

The Introduction, Chapter 1, and Chapter 2 are designed to give the reader an overview of the unique characteristics of leadership development while introducing them to some of the primary challenges of mid-life.

The Introduction will familiarize you with J. Robert Clinton's Leadership Emergence Theory (LET). This leadership development stage theory is the baseline for all three of our "Well" books. *Living and Leading Well* focuses on the ministry/leadership formation and life maturing stages while giving opportunity to evaluate the quality of our spiritual formation (inner-life growth) as the foundation for navigating mid-life challenges in such a way that we are better prepared to finish well (convergence and afterglow).

Chapter 1: Few Leaders Finish Well will describe the reality that "few leaders finish well." Many who do not finish well are taken out in mid-life because of flaws in their character that are exposed by the challenges, pressures, and crossroads of this critical stage of life.

Chapter 2: Mid-Life Challenges will introduce you to the big picture of life-long leadership development and the unique transitions and challenges that you may face in mid-life.

2. **Providing Biblical insight and opportunities to examine your spiritual formation foundation using the I Timothy 1: 5 Principle to examine potential "cracks" in your foundation that can lead to burnout, blowout, or plateauing.**

Part 1: EVALUATION will give you an opportunity to examine and evaluate your spiritual formation foundation of purity of heart, clarity of conscience, and maturing faith (I Timothy 1: 5) as it relates to growing in love and effectiveness as a person and leader.

Chapter 3: Examining Your Foundations will examine the I Timothy 1: 5 Principle and how failure to establish, maintain, and enlarge your spiritual formation foundation can make you vulnerable to burnout, blowout, and plateauing.

Chapter 4: 10 Warning Signs of Burnout will describe "intimacy cracks" in your foundation and provide opportunity for evaluation of 10 warning signs that may indicate that you are headed for burnout in life and ministry.

Chapter 5: 10 Warning Signs of Blowout will describe "integrity cracks" in your foundation and provide opportunity for evaluation for 10 warning signs that may indicate that you are headed for blowout (moral, ethical, or legal failure) in life and ministry.

Chapter 6: 10 Warning Signs of Plateauing will describe "trust cracks" in your foundation and provide opportunities for evaluation of 10 warning signs of life/ministry plateauing, which is one of the most subtle barriers to finishing well.

Chapter 7: Establishing Disciplines of Faithfulness will describe five disciplines of faithfulness and their "life renewing" significance for navigating the challenges and transitions of mid-life.

3. **Ministering to your inner life as well as provide information about life and leadership purpose through mid-life.**

Part 2: ENHANCEMENTS will focus on the practical application of Biblical principles for health and wholeness in your inner life so that you can more freely function out of the "being" reality of life and ministry.

Chapter 8: Moving Towards Focus will describe the importance of Godly vision for understanding life and leadership purpose and decision-making. Primary "attacks" on vision and Biblical antidotes will be described to help the Christian leader gain clarity and focus on God's purpose for their lives.

Chapter 9: Articulating Ministry Philosophy will explore the relationship between core values, giftedness (spiritual gifts, natural abilities, and acquired skills), and developing an effective personal philosophy of ministry for focus in fulfilling life and leadership purpose.

Chapter 10: Finding the Right Role will describe the four focal points of a focused life: purpose, role, methodologies, and ultimate contributions. Finding our right fit or role is part of understanding and walking out all four aspects of a focused life as you prepare yourself to finish well and experience fruitfulness and fulfillment in your life and leadership.

4. **Providing Biblical and real life insights and examples for navigating the challenges and embracing the opportunities of mid-life growth and ministry.**

Part 3: EMPOWERMENT will focus on the critical tasks of gaining and maintaining accountability as you begin to become more intentional about your destiny and establishing a lasting legacy as you move into convergence and afterglow.

Chapter 11: Accountability and Mentoring will describe the importance of being mentored, being a mentor for others, and accountability in successfully navigating the challenges and transitions of mid-life while preparing yourself to finish well and leave a lasting legacy.

Chapter 12: Living and Leading Well will give examples, advice, and resources for living and leading well as you navigate the challenges of mid-life and establish the necessary resources for finishing well.

It is our desire that *Living and Leading Well* will be a blessing to you. Far too many leaders today are loosing their way in mid-life. Many are dropping out of full-time ministry because of fatigue or moral compromise. Many others are loosing the joy of their "first love" relationship with Christ. We trust that God will meet you in the pages of this book and that your "strength will be renewed" and that you will better be able to "fight the good fight" so that someday you will stand before God and hear, "Well done... good and faithful servant!"

Introduction

It is the "heart" of our leadership that really matters and Jesus is the gold standard by which true leadership must be evaluated and ultimately lived out. J. Robert Clinton (*The Making of a Leader*) has studied leadership from a Bible-centered perspective for four plus decades. He and his students at Fuller seminary have case studies of over four thousand Biblical, historical, and contemporary leaders representing men and women from diverse social and cultural circumstances. From these studies, Clinton (p. 14) has developed the following definition of Biblical leadership:

> "Leadership is a dynamic process in which a man or woman with God-given capacity and God-given responsibility influences a specific group of God's people toward God's purpose for that group."

A closer look at this definition reveals that there are two *inputs* leading to two *outputs*:

1. ***God-given capacity***
2. ***God-given responsibility***

INFLUENCES

1. ***God's people***
2. ***God's purposes***

The inputs of Biblical leadership involve God-given: 1. capacity and 2. responsibility. All leaders have capacity and responsibility to influence. Capacity involves personality, life experiences, social networks, and gift mix (natural abilities, acquired skills, and spiritual gifts). These capacities can and need to be developed and maximized in the context of God's grace, because God will hold us responsible for what we do with what he has given us (see Matthew 25: 14-30).

The purpose of Biblical leadership is to partner with God in his purpose(s) to INFLUENCE others by the power of the spirit and word. *The outputs of Biblical leadership* involve: 1. God's people and 2. God's purpose(s). All people are God's people - believers and non-believers. As Bible-centered leaders we need to figure out whom it is that God wants us to influence (and for what purpose). This is usually a process of discovery which Clinton calls the "little-big" principle, "Whoever can be trusted with very little can also be trusted with much..." (Matthew 16: 10, NIV). This process of discovery and growth usually involves the following principles:

1. God develops a leader over a lifetime.

2. All Christian leaders are disciples.

3. God sovereignly uses people, circumstances, and ministry assignments to shape the life of the leader.

4. Effective ministry ("doing") comes out of a "being" relationship with God.

5. If we obey God's will, we will grow in character and influence. If we do not obey God's will, we will stagnate in character and influence.

6. Mature leadership involves an integration of spiritual formation, ministry formation, and strategic formation:

* *Spiritual Formation* – emphasis on developing intimacy with God and integrity.
* *Ministry Formation* – emphasis on identifying and developing gift mix (spiritual gifts, natural abilities, and acquired skills).
* *Strategic Formation* – emphasis on understanding and developing God's call and unique philosophy of ministry, and being intentional about accomplishing it.

The basis of kingdom influence is that "effective ministry comes out of healthy relationships with God and others" (Clinton). That is why character is addressed so thoroughly in both the Old and New Testaments as essential for effective leadership. Paul describes the qualifying characteristics of church leaders in I Timothy 3: 2-7 and Titus 1: 6-9 as they relate to choosing elders for leadership in the church.

J. Robert Clinton has based his leadership studies on the exhortation in Hebrews 13: 7 that says, "Remember your leaders, who spoke the word of God to you. Consider the outcome of their way of life and imitate their faith" (NIV). Clinton has developed his leadership emergence theory (LET), a stage theory, out of his years of studying Biblical, historical, and contemporary leaders in multiple cultures and gender roles.

This theory involves six stages (see Diagram 1) that build on one another as the Christian leader grows and matures towards fulfillment of God's ultimate purpose for his or her life. Each stage is unique in its focus and forms the basis for advancement and effectiveness in the next stage. Each stage involves processing unique God ordained circumstances in ways that lead to growth of character, maturity, and expansion of ministry.

Each of these stages provides unique challenges and opportunities to experience God in deeper ways and to grow and mature as disciples and leaders. This model of leadership development emphasizes both character (being) and competency (doing) development.

Diagram 1: General Time Line

Stage 1	Stage 2	Stage 3	Stage 4	Stage 5	Stage 6
Sovereign Foundations	Inner-life Growth	Ministry/Leadership Maturing	Life Maturing	Convergence	After Glow

We can either cooperate with God in these circumstances that lead to growth in character, maturity, and effectiveness; or we can resist God and stagnate in our growth and development as leaders. Three basic elements are involved in the process:

1. God initiates development throughout a lifetime so that we will become more Christ-like.

2. We can respond positively or negatively to God's sovereign initiation in our life.

If we respond positively, we grow in Christ-like character, maturity, effectiveness, and influence; but if we respond negatively, we will stagnate until we respond positively to the issue.These three elements form the basis for our growth, maturity, effectiveness, and influence as we progress from stage to stage in our development as Christian leaders. There is no guarantee that we will progress in our leadership development through all six stages. But it is God's intention that each one of us realizes our full potential as we grow in maturity. He has given us his son, his word, his spirit, the church, as well as a host of Biblical, historical, and contemporary examples to rely on and learn from. He wants us to learn to appropriate all that he has done for us and given us so that we might "run with perseverance the race marked out for us" (see Hebrews 12:1-3). Let's take a brief look at each of these six stages of leadership development.

Stage 1 - Sovereign Foundations

The first stage is called sovereign foundations. This stage involves God's sovereign laying of a foundation for a person's life through his or her family, social, and historical context. God places each of us in a relational and historical context that will maximize our opportunities to know him and to become the person whom he desires us to become. God's sovereign involvement in the foundational aspects of our birth, race, gender, family, culture, and historical context is described in Psalm 139: 13-16:

"For you created my inmost being; you knit me together in my mother's womb. I praise you because I am fearfully and wonderfully made; your works are wonderful, I know that full well. My frame was not hidden from you when I was made in the secret place. When I was woven together in the depths of the earth, your eyes saw my unformed body. All the days ordained for me were written in your book before one of them came to be."

God knows us! He knows everything about us. He knows of our self-centeredness and what it will take to bring us to him. He allows us to be exposed to the devastating consequences of sin in our lives, relationships, societies, and world affairs so that we will recognize our need for him. Paul describes the nature of sinful humanity in the following passage:

> "There is no one righteous, not even one; there is no one who understands, no one who seeks God. All have turned away, they have together become worthless; there is no one who does good, not even one. Their throats are open graves; their tongues practice deceit. The poison viper is on their lips. Their mouths are full of cursing and bitterness. Their feet are swift to shed blood; ruin and misery mark their ways, and the way of peace they do not know. There is no fear of God before their eyes." (Romans 3: 11-18, NIV)

He also gives us ample opportunities to know him. Even in cultures where the gospel has not yet been proclaimed, God has given a witness in creation and conscience (Romans 1:20). But in cultures such as ours, he has also given us the Bible and the witness of the church. If those who have not been exposed to the gospel are without excuse, how much more are we responsible to God for his witness to us?

Not only does God know what it will take to bring us to him, he loves us (see John 3:16) and knows of our potential to love him and become all that he has destined us to be. Each of us has a destiny to have a love relationship with God and to fulfill a specially designed role in God's plan to save a lost humanity from their sin.

The reality of God's sovereignty in these foundational matters is not meant to diminish the tragedy and heartache of broken relationships or inhumanity. God does not allow any circumstances to take place in our lives that he has not faced on our behalf (see Hebrews 4:15-16) and that he cannot use for good (see Romans 8:28). Human heartache and tragedy can become the context for growth and blessing.

Stage 2 - Inner-Life Growth

The second stage is called inner-life growth. This stage involves developing a foundational relationship with God out of which Christ-like character and maturity develop. During inner-life growth we make our initial commitment to Christ as Savior and Lord and begin to learn to relate to him in a process of life transformation.

The development of a devotional life (not a just a "time") is critical during this stage. We will want to spend time with this person who loves us so much that he gave his life that we might be set free from the bondage of our sin.

Love is a powerful reality. If you have ever been in love, been around some one in love, or wished you were in love; you know that people in love want to spend time with each other, do things with each other, and do things for each other. When we receive a letter, e-mail, phone call, or text from our loved one, we drop everything in order to hear what they have to say. When our behavior is displeasing to our loved one, we try to change it. This is the reality of our new relationship with Christ, our loved one.

The importance of an intimate relationship with God based in a healthy devotional life is well documented in Biblical, historical, and contemporary leaders who have started, stayed, and finished well.

Out of our growing relationship with God will come God initiated opportunities for the transformation of our character from being self-centered to Christ-centered. God initiates this process in the inner-life growth stage in three primary areas. These areas include integrity, obedience, and word checks:

- *Integrity checks* are special tests that God initiates to reveal the true intentions of our heart and when passed serve as a springboard for the expansion of a person's capacity to be trusted by God.

- *Obedience checks* are special tests that reveal our willingness to obey God regardless of circumstances and apparent consequences and when passed lead to the realization of God's promises.

- *Word checks* are special tests that reveal the ability to receive and understand a word from God, and allow God to work out the fulfillment of this word.

Stage 3 – Ministry/Leadership Maturing

The third stage is called ministry/leadership maturing. This stage involves developing and maturing in effective leadership through the identification and application of one's gift mix and ministry skills. This process can take place in vocational, lay ministry, and/or marketplace contexts where one can be challenged to respond positively to leadership tasks, relationships, conflicts, and authority. It is in this initial phase of ministry/leadership involvement that a person begins to discover their gift mix.

A person's gift mix is made up of a combination of spiritual gifts, natural abilities, and acquired skills. It is through the obedient (and loving) use of your gift mix that you will probably have your most rewarding and influential opportunities to impact others. Leadership skills refer to those specific skills that you acquire in leadership situations that help you to perform tasks more effectively.

An awareness of your gift mix is important, but it is in the context of leadership opportunities, ministry tasks, relationships, conflict, and submission to authority that you learn how to effectively lead and minister. Loving relationships with God and others is a priority in this stage. To accomplish a task in an unloving manner is not mature leadership. God's plans must always be accomplished God's way!

Stage 4 - Life Maturing

The fourth stage of development is life maturing. This stage involves developing a personal sense of calling and a mature Biblical philosophy of ministry/leadership.

Calling is closely associated with life purpose or your personal destiny. Calling comes from God and is usually discovered through the "little-big" principle of becoming more aware or prepared for God's ultimate purpose as you learn obedience in the here-and-now. Christian leaders must learn how to grow from "faith to faith"

(Romans 1: 15, KJV). Faithfulness over the long haul eventually leads to clarity and fulfillment of calling.

A personal and mature Biblical philosophy of ministry/ leadership is foundational for convergence in stage 5 when inner-life preparation, a person's giftedness, ministry/leadership experience, and philosophy come together in the effective and fruitful expression of one's destiny or ultimate purpose. Ministry/leadership philosophy refers to the ideas, values, and principles that a Christian uses for decision making, for exercising influence, and for evaluating self, relationships, and ministry effectiveness.

The process of developing a personal philosophy of ministry/ leadership involves three factors and three sub-stages (Table 1). The first factor is the Biblical dynamic. The basis of any mature philosophy must be the Bible. The second factor is our personal giftedness. We tend to see life and ministry/leadership through the grid of our giftedness. And the third factor is our personal experience. We tend to see reality from our own experience. Neither our giftedness or experience should contradict the Bible, but they will play a significant role in the development of our ministry/leadership philosophy.

Table 1 – Characteristics of Ministry/Leadership Philosophy

Factors	Sub-Stages
Biblical Dynamics	Osmosis
Personal Gift Mix	Baby Steps
Personal Experience	Maturity

Ministry/leadership philosophy develops over time. We have a philosophy in earlier stages, but it is not usually personal or mature. Ministry/leadership philosophy usually develops through the three sub-stages of osmosis, baby steps, and maturity. Osmosis refers to the beginning stages of developing a philosophy when we learn primarily by observation of others and by experimentation. We are attracted to someone's ministry or leadership so we try to imitate them. We read a book or go to a seminar and try to implement what we learned in our own situation.

The next sub-stage after osmosis is called baby steps. In the baby step sub-stage we learn by intentional design and evaluation. We begin to seek God for Biblical principles for life and leadership and evaluate our performance on this basis. We begin to ask questions about whether traditional or contemporary ways of doing things are necessarily God's ways.

The final sub-stage is maturity. In this stage Christian leaders are able to articulate their philosophy in terms of lifestyle. Ministry/leadership philosophy is no longer theory - it is now practical and forms the basis for decision-making, exercising influence, and evaluation.

Along with gaining clarity on calling and philosophy of ministry/leadership the Christian leader will face four major lessons that need to be learned during this stage if they are to move on to convergence:

1. Mature ministry/leadership flows out of mature character.

2. Mature character is formed through obedience in difficult situations.

3. Many Christians go through difficult situations without knowing of the potential benefits. It is important to discover God in the midst of difficult situations and learn of him.

4. Mature leaders operate with spiritual authority as their primary base of power. In this development phase, leaders learn how spiritual authority is cultivated. In essence, spiritual authority is not a goal but a byproduct of obedience. Obedience in the difficult seasons of life leads to a depth of Godly character that facilitates spiritual authority.

Stage 5: Convergence

The fifth stage of development is convergence. This stage involves the mature coming together of inner-life preparation, ministry/leadership maturing, and life maturing to fulfill your destiny or ultimate purpose.

Convergence involves the coming together of five major and five minor factors. The major factors include dependence upon God, giftedness, ministry philosophy, role, and influence. The minor factors include our experience, focus, methodology, destiny, and legacy (see Table 2). In convergence, the leader has the sense that things have come together in such a way that you are operating at your maximum potential as a leader.

Convergence involves the substantial realization of your full potential as God's beloved children and co-workers in several areas that are essential for your fulfillment as healthy and whole human beings. These include the following major and minor factors:

Table 2 - Characteristics of Convergence Stage

Major Factors	Minor Factors
Dependence on God	Life Experience
Giftedness	Focus
Ministry Philosophy	Methodology
The Right Role	Destiny
Appropriate Influence	Legacy

Stage 6 – Afterglow

The final stage is afterglow. This stage is characterized by the enjoyment and influence available to a person who has substantially completed their life calling or destiny. This stage is rarely attained (in part because so few leaders finish well), but when convergence has been realized and God grants additional years to a Christian leader they can continue to have major influence through their relationship with others. The primary tasks in this stage are to finish well and pass the baton of leadership on to the next generation.

Spiritual mentoring can be a major influence role in this stage and have a profound impact on younger leaders. The establishing of a lasting legacy through the mentoring of others in their life challenges is very important in afterglow. This is a stage in which a Christian leader is able to enjoy the blessings of a life of obedience. From the status of finishing well comes encouragement and influence for the next generations of disciples and leaders to also do what it takes to finish well.

Context and Conclusion

A basic understanding of Clinton's leadership emergence theory (LET) will serve as the framework for the following chapters. The focus of this book will be on the mid-life stages of ministry/leadership maturing (gift mix development) and life maturing (discovering calling and developing ministry philosophy), but we will also make reference to the inner-life growth stage because of its importance for developing our spiritual formation foundation. Cracks in your foundation begin to become more noticeable in mid-life and unless you address them you may find yourselves burning out, blowing out, or plateauing.

This book is designed to help you build strong foundations which can stand the weight and pressures of mid-life while helping prepare you to finish well and establish a lasting legacy.

Chapter 1

Few Leaders Finish Well

The first time I (Richard) heard God challenging me about finishing well I was in my first ten years of ministry. I had learned about the dangers, traps, and pitfalls that blocked many leaders from finishing well from my father's research, but I was sure that this did not apply to me. I was filled with inspiration to finish well and I thought I had a really clear vision of what my finish would look like. I found it easy to imagine what my accomplishments would be.

At present, nearly 30 years into ministry and 20 years beyond my initial responses to the idea of finishing well, things are not as clear as they once were. I have not given up on the challenge to finish well. In fact, I would say that my resolve to finish well is much stronger now, but I have been tested during these middle years and have found them more challenging than I ever imagined.

The Marathon of Life and Leadership

I have never run in a marathon, but I lived through this experience vicariously with my older sister. It was an incredible experience to be with her on the day of the marathon. My respect and admiration for everyone who runs marathons is quite high after seeing a race firsthand. The runners who impressed me the most were like my sister who was tackling this challenge for the first time.

Every runner had to overcome the physical challenge of running such a long distance. They had to deal with the elements that on this day included cold temperatures and very windy conditions. Along with these, my sister described the emotional challenge and the psychological challenge she also expected to face.

I learned from talking to several of the runner before the race that they each had certain goals in mind before the race started. Once the race began, all the runners began to set a pace that would lead them to their goals. I ran the first several miles with my sister. It was incredible to feel the energy from all the other runners and to see how things developed. My brother in law, my niece, and I took turns running along with my sister. I noticed over the course of the race that the toughest part of the race was the middle miles. I watched the psychological and emotional battle raging on the faces of the runners. Many of the runners dropped out during this stage.

Then at some point about two-thirds into the race, there was a resolve, a determination that came on the faces of many of the remaining runners. Maybe they were still on pace or maybe they were behind or ahead of their pace. No matter where they were, you could tell the goal now was to finish. You could tell that the runners were trying to overcome the physical and psychological challenges of getting their bodies and minds to submit to their goal of finishing.

My brother in law and niece ran with my sister the last several miles of the race so I had the chance to go to the finish line. The winners of the race had long since crossed the line as several hundred additional runners cross the line. Those of us watching the finish line cheered and cheered for every one of them. What was especially touching was the fact that many of the runners who had finished earlier had now gathered together to cheer for the other runners.

Finishing the Race

Every person that crossed that line won that day. It was an extremely emotional moment for many of the runners. I loved being there. I was so proud of my sister when she came across that line. This experience of watching my sister run the marathon has influenced my perspective on what it means to finish well as a Christian leader. While I may never run in a marathon (bad knees from too many years of soccer), I am in the midst of a long race. Several years ago, I committed myself to being a Christian leader and began my race. During the first ten years of ministry, there were many obstacles to overcome and I had to battle through a lot of challenges.

The last twenty years of ministry have taken their toll. Many of the people that I started in ministry with all those years ago are no longer operating in ministry leadership roles. I have seen many dreams, visions, hopes, and desires crash and burn. Many of my own dreams and visions have not come to pass like I imagined that they would. I have been involved in a number of near fatal crashes myself.

But by the grace of God, I am still in the race. I am still fighting, struggling, and running the race with endurance that God has laid out for me. I still have a passion for the things of God and I want to finish well. The finish line is a little closer than it was all those years ago and I can see more clearly what it will take to finish well.

As I begin the process of writing this book, I have to admit that I feel a bit intimidated by the task. As I grow older, I find that I have less and less energy to pretend. I have a passion for truth and honesty. I don't want to misrepresent myself by making it sound like I have everything together and I am some super leader. The truth is simple. I have been in ministry now for about 30 years and I am working hard to keep going...just like every other leader. But many years ago, the Lord asked me to share my heart and my life with others. So I will endeavor to share some things I have picked up along the way in the hopes that some of these things will encourage you and help you.

How Does an Enemy Think?

I have had the privilege of being involved in the process of training many different leaders in several different settings. I love to see how God develops his leaders and I get excited when I can be a part of what he is doing. It is truly one of the great joys in my life. In these settings, I have often challenged these leaders with the issue of finishing well. I have quoted the frightening statistics from my father's research that only about one in four Christian leaders finish well. I have plenty of stories about leaders who have crashed and burned which adds a realistic dimension to the challenge. The Biblical evidence is pretty overwhelming. There are just not very many leaders who make it to the end and finish well.

I have observed that people respond differently to this challenge. Some rise to the challenge and proclaim, "I will be one of those who finishes well!" Others think, "if so many leaders do not make it, what chance do I have?" The wise leaders respond, "What will give me the best chance of finishing well? What can I do to increase my chances?"

I ask every leader to be honest with themselves, their fellow leaders, and with God. Then I make the following challenge, "You know yourself very well. Look at the following barriers to finishing well that kept the leaders in the Bible from finishing well. Think like the enemy of God. Which of these areas would you use to attack yourself? Which of these areas is the weakest in your life and which attack would have the best chance of succeeding?"

6 Barriers to Finishing Well

Barrier 1.	Problems with finances
Barrier 2.	The abuse of power (often called spiritual abuse)
Barrier 3.	Wrongful pride
Barrier 4.	Sexual misconduct
Barrier 5.	Unhealthy family relationships and problems
Barrier 6.	Plateauing (the stopping of development and growth)

Then I ask these leaders to think about this some more and then we share our answers with one another. Many leaders have a difficult time being honest and it is difficult to share weaknesses with other leaders. As a result of this, the most popular answer is always plateauing. I remember one time listening to other leaders share their answers and I began to think about my own. I was nearly wiped out and taken out of ministry as I went through a painful divorce. For me, the barrier of unhealthy family relationships is a big one.

I remember God speaking to me during this exercise and pointing out that the enemy could attack me in every one of the barriers. And the enemy would succeed unless I learned to build some defenses and learn to defend myself. I had to admit to myself that I was vulnerable to every kind of attack. I had to be honest with myself and begin to take steps to build defenses against attacks in each one of these areas. I especially realized that one of the real signs of plateauing is when I am not really willing to be honest with God, myself, and appropriate others.

In the challenge to stay faithful during the middle stages of life and leadership, there are some common traps that we must avoid if we are going to make it through this part of the race. These traps are different aspects of the barriers that we have listed already. I will mention several of the traps that I have found common to most leaders.

1. The Loss of Courage

A few years ago I was skiing in the Alps with one of my sons. I had learned to ski while I was in college. As I was trying to keep up with my son, I remembered that I used to ski just like him. No fear... full speed... lots of risk... high adrenaline! Now many years later, my skiing skills are much better, however, I have noticed that I have lost my courage. I am just not willing to take the same risks that I took 20 years earlier. As I skied, I was constantly telling myself to slow down and not take so many chances.

I know that there are a lot of people who never lose their sense of adventure. They are taking more risks now than when they were younger, but it has been my observation that most leaders are not willing to take as many risks after 10 or 15 years of ministry as they were at the beginning. This is true even though their ministry and leadership skills may be much better now than they were earlier on.

Joshua faced a huge challenge later in his life (see Joshua 1). Moses was gone and the burden of leadership had fallen on his shoulders. God spoke to him in this moment of transition and said, "Be strong and have courage." What is courage? The dictionary defines courage as the quality of mind or spirit that enables a person to face difficulty, danger, or pain with firmness and without fear. We call this bravery. Joshua responded to God's challenge with courage and God used him mightily.

If we are going to make it through the middle stages of the race, then we need to be "strong and courageous." As we grow older, and hopefully wiser, we will learn to discern between being courageous and foolish. Some risks are just not wise to take. But we must guard against the loss of courage. Fear is the main enemy of courage. When we allow our fears to block our ability to respond to God with courage, we are headed for difficulties and the danger of not finishing the race.

2. Drifting into Complacency

When I was first starting out in ministry, I was very uncomfortable speaking in front of groups of people. I was introverted and preferred to let other people take the speaking parts. But as God led me into increasing responsibilities as a leader, I was forced to speak to groups more and more often. Every time I spoke to a group I felt a kind of inner desperation (which I tried to hide from others). This desperation created a strong need for me to get into the presence of God and find out what he wanted to say to the group. If God did not speak to me in my preparation time, then I really struggled. However, the more speaking that I did, the more comfortable I became. I began to enjoy myself more and more. My skills as a communicator began to grow. Now after many years of speaking in many different settings, I cannot even remember what it felt like to be uncomfortable and I have lost that sense of desperation. Now, when I go into a situation where I speak, it almost always reminds me of somewhere else I have spoken.

As a speaker, I get asked to speak about similar themes such as leadership and leadership development. The temptation is to rely on the things that I know and have said before. The danger is not asking God what he wants to say. I can easily rely or place my dependence on what I have done before. Sometimes when I ask God what I should say and he says, "Share the things I have given you before." But the important thing is that I ask God what is on his heart for the people I am sharing with. I want to avoid the trap of complacency.

Complacency leads us to shift our dependency from God to our own abilities. God wants us to use and develop our abilities, but he does not want us to ever lose our sense of dependency on him. Our sense of dependency is something that we have the responsibility of cultivating. We cannot be passive in this area if we want to finish the race.

3. Burning Out

Paul will be addressing this issue in greater detail in a later chapter, but it is important to mention it at this point. Psychologically, emotionally, physically, and spiritually we must guard ourselves against getting burned out. Burning out in life and leadership is directly linked to moving ahead of God and doing things in our own strength or falling behind God and trying to catch up in our own strength. The key here is to follow the model of Jesus and learn to only do the things that the Father is doing (John 5:19-20).

4. Busyness

A number of years ago, Charles Kridiotis, a friend of mine who leads a church in Sweden, told me something that I have never forgotten. We were talking about avoiding burnout and being tired. He shared something an older pastor in South Africa had told him. The old pastor said, "If the devil can't get you to stop obeying God then he will try to keep you so busy doing the non important things so that you will never get to the important things."

When I heard this, I knew it was true for me. Busyness is one of the real issues that we have to overcome. Today, there are so many options, so much information, so many possibilities and opportunities that it can be overwhelming. We are constantly being bombarded with important messages, "You need this." "You have to do that." "Hurry! Hurry! Hurry!" "Come here." "Go there." " Push! Push! Run!"

I have spoken to hundreds of leaders and asked them what is the biggest problem that they face in ministry. Nearly all of them say the same thing, "I don't have enough time. I can't get everything done." Then I think of the old pastor from South Africa and I once again realize how true his words were.

If we are going to learn how to live and lead well, we are going to have to deal with the issue of busyness. The secret of dealing with busyness is simple, but many people just find it impossible. What is the simple solution? Just say "no!" Actually, this is only half the solution. We need to learn to say "no" to the wrong things and "yes" to the right things. We say "yes" to the things that move us forward and keep us on track towards accomplishing God's purposes for our lives and "no" to the things that distract us and keep us from focusing on the important things.

5. Becoming Disillusioned and the Sting of Cynicism

"Why am I still doing this?" "Why doesn't it work?" "Where are you God and what are you doing?" "Why isn't God doing more?" Have you ever asked yourself these kinds of questions? If we are honest, most of us have asked these kinds of questions as we face the disappointments, hurts, and criticisms that come with leadership. If you have asked yourself these kinds of questions, then you have wrestled with disillusionment.

We have an enemy who would truly love to get us to back down on our faith and our commitment to God. In order to do this, he tries to challenge us into moving from discouragement to disillusionment, and eventually into cynicism. Have you ever been tempted? Yes, of course you have. We all have to face this trap and fight our way through. Disillusionment is one of the main reasons why leaders quit the race.

I did some research on the issue of life changes and transitions and discovered that there are very natural sociological barriers that leaders need to work through as they grow and develop. In adulthood, these transitions are cyclical and occur about every 8-10 years. It is very natural and healthy to ask the deep questions during these times. Every time of transition allows us to evaluate our beliefs, our convictions, and our assumptions. These transitions provide a time to see if our reality matches the dreams, hopes, desires, and expectations.

Christian leaders go through these transitions or boundaries as well. Healthy leaders go through these times of evaluation and reflection and make adjustments to their thinking, attitudes, and behaviors. They usually struggle significantly during these times and may ask deep and challenging questions about what God is up to. I do not believe that this process threatens God. The books of Job and Habakkuk give us examples of leaders who were asking the deep questions and how God meets them. Times of transition can truly test our faith and reveal our deepest convictions.

Whenever we face situations that we cannot understand, situations that we cannot control, or situations where we are criticized, we face a moment of decision. Which direction will we turn? Will we let discouragement lead us towards disillusionment and cynicism or will we turn into the heart of God and seek him?

6. Forgetting That God Gets All the Glory

When I was a kid, my afternoons had certain rhythm. I came home from school and dropped everything inside the front door and then ran back out to play with all the neighborhood kids. Most of the time, my friends and I would play whatever sport was in season. The format was always the same. Two kids would be chosen as the captains and then they would decide who got to pick first and choose the teams. Because I was good in most sports, I was often one of the first choices. The captain was lucky to have me on their team.

Many years later, during a worship time, I found myself thinking about how lucky God was that I was on his team. I was a great addition to the Kingdom of God. I had so much that I could contribute. What a crazy (and dangerous) thought! I would have never said something so silly out loud. But I had thought it. And worse, at some deep level, I believed it to be true.

As I stood there, I was embarrassed. How could I be so proud? Then the Holy Spirit spoke to me and said, "At least you are honest. Richard, always remember that ministry is all about me. You have your abilities and skills because I created you and gave them to you. You have the opportunities to do ministry because I opened the doors for you. I deserve all the glory and I won't share my glory with anyone." In that moment, I realized that in my immaturity, I had forgotten this basic fact.

Jesus told the Pharisees on one occasion that they should not be so proud of the fact that they were children of Abraham. God could make the rocks children of Abraham if he wanted to. Ouch! What a blow to their pride. Pride shows up in many different ways. Sometimes, we rely on our own ability without involving God. Sometimes, we try to tell God what to do and how to do it (usually in a nice Christian sounding prayer). Sometimes, when we receive the praise, adoration, and strokes that come from people that we have been ministering to, we do not reflect that praise and point to God. We take a little of it in for ourselves.

When we forget that leadership and ministry are all about him and that he deserves ALL the glory and honor, we have crossed into some very dangerous territory. This is a subtle form of pride. If we have pride because of our immaturity, God will deal with us by leading us to the truth. He will show us in many ways that he is God and we are not. However, after we have been in leadership and ministry for a while, God reacts in a different way. He breaks down our pride. Sometimes this can be a painful and difficult experience. Humility is a necessary ingredient for living and leading well as we prepare ourselves to finishing well.

7. A Lack of Discipline

Some people love discipline and others do not. I am kind of in the middle. In some things I am very disciplined and in other things I am very undisciplined. One thing I have learned is that discipline does not just happen. Even if we love discipline, we have to stay focused, pay attention, and learn how to be disciplined. In order to live and lead well, learning to be disciplined is non-negotiable. Every leader needs discipline. Paul, in I Corinthians 9:24-27, tells us that he worked hard at disciplining himself. He did not want to fall down or quit in the middle of his life and ministry. He wanted to finish well.

Have you ever seen a person quit when they were close to the finish line? I do not want to be one of those people. That means I need discipline. Primarily, we need discipline in our spiritual lives. We can structure our time with God in many different ways. What we must not do is allow this time to slip away or become stagnant. A large percentage of leaders allow their time with God to just slip away or become mundane. A lack of discipline in this area can be fatal to finishing well. We need to discipline ourselves to stay focused on the mission God has given us. There are so many distractions and opportunities to move off the track that God has prepared for us. It is so easy to get caught up in the unimportant things. We need discipline to keep our attitudes, actions, and values focused on the things of God. The spiritual disciplines help us a great deal in these areas. We need to learn to discipline our bodies and take care of our health.

I have learned that there are many things in life that I have no control over and there are some things that I can control. I want to be disciplined in the things in life where I can exercise control. This allows me the best possible chance of finishing well and enjoying the abundant life that Jesus promised in John 10. Experiencing the abundant life makes all the discipline worth it.

How Will You Finish?

Have you ever committed yourself to some goal or project and then run out of steam before you completed it? I think this is a normal aspect of life. We all experience this to some degree. Some will give up on their goals and projects at this point, but those who want to finish well find a way through. Have you ever experienced a rededication? As I think about finishing well, I need to remember that I do not know what challenges will face me along the way. More than likely, I am going to face challenges that seem too great to overcome. It is at these moments where I need to rededicate myself again to God and finishing well.

Each year, I have the habit of evaluating how life is going and what things I am satisfied with and what things I am not satisfied with. I ask God to speak to me and help me understand where I am, what issues are most important, and which ones need some attention. I have several mentoring relationships and my mentors help me evaluate and hold me accountable. This activity naturally leads me to moments of recommitment or rededication. I have built these times into my normal rhythm of life and leadership because I am serious about finishing well. My question to you is quite simple:

Are you living and leading well? How are you doing in the middle part of your marathon?

Evaluation and Application:

1. How are you doing in the middle of your race? Are you tempted to quit? Are you feeling some pain, fatigue, or frustration?

2. How has the enemy been attacking you and trying to get you to quit the race?

3. What things have you done to shore up your defenses?

4. Which one of the traps mentioned (loss of courage, complacency, burnout, busyness, disillusionment, pride, or lack of discipline) have you experienced? What have you or are you learning about how to work through it?

5. How did or is God getting you freed up so that you can continue to run with greater freedom and confidence?

Chapter 2

Mid-Life Challenges

In the mid-1990s I (Paul) attended a ReFocus Facilitator's training seminar led by Terry Walling. I was in my early forties and in the third year of teaching at a Bible college located in the Pacific Northwest. During the seminar I did my first ever "post-it note" time-line. I still remember the yellow, blue, and pink post-it notes all over the table in front of me. Over time these random notes began to take the form of a time-line of my life and leadership.

Through this process several patterns and insights began to emerge. Some of them were encouraging and some were not. One that jumped out at me was my "3-4 years and out" pattern of vocation and ministry. I was aware of this pattern but had not given it a lot of thought.

Dying Hard in My Forties

As I prayerfully examined my time-line, this pattern stood out as a potential problem. There had been a couple of moves for "professional" reasons while I was climbing the ladder as a college administrator and, later after I had transitioned into vocational ministry, there were a couple of moves because of ministry conflict. I was currently in a great ministry situation, but I was restless.

Not only was I restless, but also there was growing tension in my marriage and the moves had also taken a toll on my three kids. The moves (some across country) had produced insecurity in my wife and instability for my kids. I was beginning to feel trapped in a pattern that I had rationalized as "the way I am" and now God seemed to be putting his finger on it.

As I continued to pray and try to listen to God about this over the weeks that followed, I became aware of some very disturbing issues in my life. First of all, I was in denial about the negative impact of my "3-4 years and out" pattern on my wife and family. I was being selfish and not giving up my life as an act of love for my wife and kids. My marriage and family were nearing a major crisis and I did not have a clue!

Second, I had rationalized my pattern on the basis of my personality, gifts, and vision for my life. I was good at fixing broken programs or dysfunctional teams. I had come into challenging situations again and again and turned them around in 2-3 years. I was consistently on schedule and under budget. But by the third year in a position, I had pushed the limits of the organization to a point where others were satisfied with the changes while I was just getting started.

I was now becoming aware of my efficiency at the expense of relationships. This insight made me very uneasy, as I knew that relationships were important to God. Not only this but God was beginning to reveal to me the core issue related to my pattern; and how, if I did not let him deal with me in this area, I would disqualify myself from his best purposes for my life and ministry.

The third insight was that the core issue that God wanted to deal with was the fact that I was a fleshly leader and he wanted to transform me into a spiritual leader. God revealed to me that I could make it happen for 2-3 years in the power of my personality, drive, and natural abilities. My solution for dealing with challenges was always to work harder and smarter. This seemed to serve me well, at least for awhile, but after 2-3 years of this I found myself tired, frustrated, restless, and looking for a way out ("the next challenge").

God also revealed to me that I needed to allow him to deal with this pattern before I destroyed my marriage, my family, and our future. I could make it happen for 2-3 years in the flesh, but as I began to wind down, God began to put his finger on my selfishness. Instead of submitting to God's process of killing my flesh, I would move on to take on the next challenge and abort God's process. The problem with this was that I was going in circles. I was caught in a destructive and unfulfilling pattern.

I decided that I had to change and gave God permission to kill my flesh so that I could be free from this destructive pattern. I wanted desperately to become a spiritual leader in my marriage, family, and ministry. By God's grace and the support of others, I submitted to the process and over time have experienced the breaking of this pattern at the core that has resulted in peace and contentment (that I had never experienced before) as well as a growing capacity to "abide" in Christ (resulting in not just fruit, but "much" fruit)!

The Necessity of Transformation

I have since learned that this process has been identified and described by others as "union life," the "exchanged life," the "new covenant," "resurrection life," the "victorious Christian life," etc. A study of these concepts of transformation has helped me better understand the process and its purposes.

This process has not been easy for me. My flesh has died hard. There have been embarrassing times when the flesh acted up and I struggled through tantrums and self-pity. This process was (and still is) not pretty and at times very painful, but necessary! I have learned that "if you're not broken, you're not much good to the Kingdom of God."

There is light at the end of the tunnel, and it is not an oncoming train. God is more than able to do the work of transformation needed if we will submit long enough for him to do his liberating work. Remember, that few leaders finish well. The stories of leaders and their failures are tragic, but we can learn from the tragedy of others. We do not have to repeat their failures. We are not left on our own to try and figure this stuff out. We have the Bible, the power of God, and others to help us so that we do not have to fail.

I like the title of Clinton's first research article on finishing well, "Listen Up Leaders! Forewarned is Forearmed!" If we know the barriers and the landscapes of mid-life; and if we are confident that the Bible, the power of God, and healthy support are sufficient for our victory; then we can face the responsibilities and challenges of mid-life and learn to live and lead well.

The Landscape of Mid-Life

Just because we seemed to start well in life and leadership does not mean that we will necessarily live and lead well or finish well. There is no "cruise control" in life that guarantees us success. We must live a life of honesty and openness before God and others on an ongoing basis if we are going to make it over the long haul.

King David did not wake up from his nap (II Samuel 11: 2) and decide to sabotage his life, ruin his reputation, and destroy his family and legacy by having a one-night stand. No, he had gradually let his guard down and given in to his self-life. It appears that David had gradually put his life on cruise control (see II Samuel 8: 14).

I remember a sermon that I heard as a college student entitled, "Nibbling Yourself Lost." The message was about how the lost sheep got lost (Matthew 18: 10-14). The preacher noted that the sheep did not intend to get lost, but became so focused on eating that he lost his focus on the shepherd and the rest of the flock. The sheep literally "nibbled himself" lost.

That is probably what happened to David. Over time he let down his guard. After all, God was with him and gave him victory in every battle. If we are not careful, we can gradually begin to take God for granted. We can gradually become lax in our devotional times or begin to become pragmatic about the decisions we make. We, too, can nibble ourselves lost like David did.

We must be careful! We may have started well like David did, but yesterdays foundation may not be strong enough to hold the weight of today's responsibilities and challenges. Mid-life responsibilities and challenges will expose the weaknesses of our foundation.

Our foundation is the result of our cooperation with God in establishing a spiritual formation that establishes intimacy with God, integrity, and maturing faith. This foundation must be established, maintained, and expanded as we mature in our relationship with Christ. If we are lax in our spiritual formation, cracks will begin to form in our foundation that will eventually be exposed and exploited by the weight of expanded responsibilities and challenges that come with mid-life. Some of these responsibilities and challenges include:

- **Aging issues** – we are getting older and probably a little fatter. We may be facing health, expectation, and image issues that challenge our sense of worth and quality of life.

- **Professional/Ministry issues** – we are getting older and may feel that we are running out of time related to earlier hopes, dreams, and goals. We may feel trapped by our circumstances and responsibilities.

- **Marital issues** – we have probably been married for several years now and are facing the challenges of keeping our marriages alive, changing sexual drives, teenagers, empty nest, planning for retirement, etc.

- **Family issues** – we have probably faced the challenges of raising children. There may have been some drama during the teenage years and possibly one or more of our children are not following Christ. We may also be caught in between by having to also care for aging parents.

- **Personal issues** – we may be struggling through a "mid-life crisis" of identity. We may have to navigate unexpected crises of identity, relationships, and work. We may discover things about ourselves that we do not like and demand major changes.

- **Inner Life issues** – we may find ourselves getting sick and tired of being sick and tired. We have worked as hard as we possibly can and have not experienced the quality of life that we had hoped for. Over time, we may have become human doings rather than human beings. We may have lost the balance of fruitfulness out of abiding (John 15: 5).

- **Character issues** – we may have become so busy and overwhelmed with the demands and responsibilities of life that we have begun to cut corners and make pragmatic choices that have begun to compromise our integrity. We may be a little alarmed or even convicted but these are "little things" and we are so busy that we just need to "go with the flow."

Any one of these issues can be challenging enough, but in mid-life many of these seem to come at us at the same time. It can be overwhelming!

It's a Battlefield Out There!

Not only do we contend in life with natural, moral, and spiritual issues like these, but we also must learn to contend with spiritual warfare (Ephesians 6: 10-20). We have an enemy who "prowls around like a roaring lion looking for someone to devour" (I Peter 5: 8).

As leaders, we are especially vulnerable because of our higher profile and our influence on others. In the Revolutionary War the patriots developed an effective strategy against the more equipped British forces. They shot the officers! Even though the patriots were less equipped, this strategy was very effective. They learned that if you take out leaders, you discourage followers.

This strategy reminds me of one of my favorite Farside cartoons that I have posted on a bookcase in my office as a reminder. The cartoon shows two buck deer with antlers (probably just before hunting season) standing on their hind feet facing one another. You see the back of one and the front of the other. The one who's front you see has a bulls eye on its chest and the one who's back you see is saying, "Bummer of a birthmark, Hal!" What a picture of the reality of leadership and its vulnerabilities!

Forewarned is Forearmed!

If it could happen to David, it could happen to you or me. How we process the challenges of mid-life will determine the quality of the remainder of our lives and leadership. Will we suck it up and keep pushing through hoping that we do not burn out, blow out, or plateauing in the process? Or, will we take the time needed to allow God to reveal the strength and weakness of our spiritual foundation and make the necessary changes so that we can live and lead well while we prepare to finish well?

It is during our mid-life years that we determine how we will finish and the legacy that we will leave. What will the answer be for you and me? Our answer will make all the difference. "Listen Up Leaders! Forewarned is Forearmed!"

Evaluation and Application

1. Do you have any patterns that God may want to break in your life so that you can become more free and effective in life and leadership? What are they? How does God want you to partner with him in this process?

2. Prayerfully think about David and his fall. What can you learn from David and how do you intend to keep from repeating his experience?

3. Which of the mid-life challenges are you facing? How are you doing with them? Do you have anybody who you can talk to and pray with about these challenges? If not, what is your plan for connecting with the right person or people who can support you during this season of your life?

4. What is your understanding of spiritual warfare? Read and study Ephesians 6: 10-20 and evaluate whether you have all of your spiritual armor on. If not, what equipment or weapon do you need to appropriate and how do you plan to do this?

Chapter 3

Examining Your Foundations

What a day! I (Paul) had just broken up a verbal confrontation between two of my children's ministry leaders in a busy hallway during the morning service. Tensions, frustrations, and bad vibes had been simmering for months, but had never boiled over in public. I calmed folks down, put the best spin on the situation that I could, and escaped to my office to regroup.

I had been serving as an Associate Pastor/Director of Educational Ministries at a church of about 5,000 for over a year. My responsibilities involved hands on oversight of children's ministry (which involved about 1,000 children, 150 adult volunteers, and 15 part-time paid leaders), resource leader for youth ministries, and director of an adult training center (which involved about 1,000 students per year). Children's ministry had been a real challenge because it was under resourced and the few committed people were overworked and stressed out.

I had used all of my management and administrative skills to organize the ministry. We had job descriptions, policies and procedures, guidelines, staff meetings with agendas, etc. But all of this was not enough!

God's Tool Box

So I found myself in my office overwhelmed with a sense of hopelessness. I had tried everything that I knew about organizing people for success (most of which had worked well in other settings), but it was not working here. While I sat in my office behind my desk I had an "impression" (a picture in my head) of me sitting in my office with a fancy toolbox on my desk and Jesus sitting on the other side of the desk.

In the impression, Jesus looked at me and asked if he could take a look at my toolbox. I said, "Sure!" as I was apparently pretty proud of my toolbox and thought Jesus would be impressed. Jesus took the toolbox off of my desk, put it on the floor, opened it, and began to examine my tools. He took each tool out individually and threw it over his shoulder saying, "This will never do!" When he finished throwing away all of my tools he closed the toolbox and placed in on my desk saying, "Now you're ready!"

New Tools

I wish I could have been more spiritual in my impression, but I was not. I responded, "What do you mean 'I'm ready.' You just threw away all of my tools?" As I watched myself say this I began to realize that I had invested my life in collecting the wrong tools for the task that God was calling me to. I began to pray and ask God what the tools were that I needed to accomplish his purposes. As I prayed I sensed God saying that his tools for me needed to be love (for him and others), prayer (and fasting), and perseverance.

I must be honest here. I was busted by this encounter with God. I had invested in tools that made me competent, but not effective (in a Kingdom of God sense). I felt so naked and exposed. As I confessed (agreed with God) that I had invested in the wrong tools (not that many of the skills that I learned in management are not useful, they just are not enough) I began to sense that God was leading me to make some radical changes in my life and leadership.

Out of a time of wrestling over the implications of this "impression" and a growing sense of direction from God I committed to prayer and fasting for children's ministry people every Friday. I would need to visit every classroom and meeting room, and pray for the leaders, teachers, and children (and parents in some cases). It would take me between 4-8 hours. At first I resisted because I was so busy, but eventually God wore me down and I began to implement this new strategy. I sensed that God gave me some key Bible passages (Malachi 4: 5-6, Luke 18: 15-17, Luke 19: 45-46) to pray through during these times.

It was a lot of hard work and not very effective at first. In fact, things seemed to get worse. The tensions, frustration, and bad vibes that had characterized children's ministry in the past did not go away overnight. In fact, it took about six months of persevering prayer before the first breakthrough happened. It happened during a Sunday morning staff meeting before our early morning service.

Breakthrough

By that time I had developed a strategy of meeting by agenda to keep my staff from fighting with one another. We would meet at a prescribed time each Sunday and I would lead the staff through the agenda and then we would pray before going to our areas of ministry responsibility. During one of these meetings one of my staff began to weep and asked me if he could say something. I allowed him to speak and he began to share that he was ambitious, competitive, and judgmental toward other staff and asked them to forgive him. This lead to several others confessing similar issues and also asking for forgiveness. It was the beginning of a new day in children's ministry.

A few weeks later, my staff informed me that during the week leading up to the deadline for volunteer workers for children's ministry that more volunteers than we needed had applied (and many of them shared that they were making open ended commitments out of a sense of calling). This had never happened before. Throughout my tenure we had always had to manipulate people to work with children and we never had enough volunteers.

A few weeks later, during the worship time for the 4th-6th graders we experienced an unusual "visitation" of God. The children began to spontaneously dance and hold hands in a widening circle. Our adult staff, teachers, and volunteers watched on with amazement when suddenly the children stopped and began to take the hands of adults and include us in their worship. For a brief time many of us experienced the "faith of a child" that I had been praying for.

Out of this new culture, a sense of community and creativity emerged. We began to equip our children for ministry as members of worship teams, prayer teams, and visitation teams. Children began to write worship songs, they prayed powerfully for others, and visited local children's hospitals to minister to patients and their families. And I was able to train a team of people who no longer needed my leadership and took this ministry to the next level.

This experienced introduced me to the reality that effective ministry comes out of a "being" relationship with God and others. Competence is essential in life and leadership, but it is not enough in and of itself. We need something more.

The I Timothy 1: 5 Principle

As a result of my "God's tool box" experience I became more aware of the simple, profound, and difficult task of becoming a person who lives and ministers out of love. In Matthew 22: 37-40, we are reminded of the over-ridding reality of love. Jesus said:

> "'Love the Lord your God with all your heart and with all your soul and with all your mind.' This is the first and greatest commandment. And the second is like it: 'Love your neighbor as yourself.' All the Law and the Prophets hang on these two commandments." (NIV)

Love God and love your neighbor - a brilliant idea, but not so easy to do. My struggles with the application of this passage have led me to a careful study of the Bible concerning love which in turn has led me to discover what I call the I Timothy 1: 5 Principle. This passage says:

> "The goal of this command is love, which comes from a pure heart and a good conscience and a sincere faith." (NIV)

The Mark of the Christian

Francis Schaeffer calls love the "mark of the Christian." It is to be the distinguishing characteristic of true followers of Christ. There are many ideas about what love is in our culture: "Is love a feeling?" "Do we fall in love?" [which means that we can fall out of love!] "If you love me, you would know how to meet my needs!" "Make love not war!" You have heard these uses of the word love and many more. What does love really mean, what does it look like?

I Corinthians 13 - Love

"If I speak in the tongues of men and angels… If I have the gift of prophecy and can fathom all mysteries and all knowledge… if I have a faith that can move mountains… If I give all I possess to the poor and surrender my body to the flames, **but have not love, I gain nothing.**" I Corinthians 13: 1-3 (NIV, **bold** added for emphasis)

Love in the Bible

Here is a very brief overview of what the Bible teaches about love. There is much more in the Bible, but the following list will serve as a general framework for understanding what love is suppose to be like:

- God is love – I John 4: 8
- God's love is manifest in redemption – John 3: 16
- Jesus demonstrates God's love by dying for our sins – John 15: 13
- We can love because God loves us – I John 4: 19
- We are to love God with all our mind, heart, soul, strength – Matthew 22: 37
- We have the fruit of the Spirit as part of our salvation – Galatians 5: 22
- We demonstrate love through obedience to God – I John 2: 5

- We are to love one another – I John 4: 7
- We are to love our neighbors – Matthew 22: 39
- We are to love the poor and needy – Luke 10: 29-37
- We are to love our enemies – Luke 6: 27

Definition of Love (agape) – "Christian love has God as its primary object, and expresses itself first of all in obedience to his commandments... Self-will, that is self-pleasing, is the negative of love of God... Christian love is not an impulse from the feelings; it does not always run with natural inclinations... Love seeks the welfare of all (Romans 15: 2) and works no ill to any (Romans 13: 8-10); love seeks opportunity to do good to all (Galatians 6: 10)... [it is part of the] fruit of the Spirit (Galatians 6: 22), [it is the primary characteristic] of God (I John 4: 8), [and is the primary means] for ministry (I Corinthians 13: 1-3)" (adapted from *Vine's Complete Expository Dictionary*).

After the introduction of love in I Corinthian 13, the passage goes on to describe in great detail what love really is and what it should look like:

> "Love is patient, love is kind. It does not envy, it does not boast, it is not proud. It is not rude, it is not self-seeking, it is not easily angered, it keeps no record of wrongs. Love does not delight in evil but rejoices with truth. It always protects, always trusts, always hopes, always perseveres. Love never fails."(*I* Corinthians 13: 4-8, NIV)

Let's take a more in depth look at each of these words and phrases in order to gain a clearer understanding of the Biblical reality of love:

- Patient (*makrothumia*) – "long suffering"
- Kind (*chrestotes*) – "goodness of heart, serviceable, pleasant"
- Does not envy (*zeloo*) – "indignation, jealousy [to have what others have]"
- Does not boast (*perpereuomai*) – "to vaunt oneself, vainglory, brag"
- Is not proud (*phusioo*) – "to puff up, blow up, inflate [with pride]"
- Is not rude (*aschnmomai*) – "to act unbecomingly [at the expense of others]"
- Is not self-seeking (*zeteo*) – "to strive after, endeavor, desire [self]"
- Is not easily angered (*orge*) – "gradual, long lasting anger"
- Does not keep a record of wrongs (*kakos*) –"injurious, destructive [hurtful]"
- Does not delight in evil (*adikeo*) – "unrighteousness, to do wrong"
- Rejoices with truth (*alethes*) – "real, ideal, genuine"
- Always protects (*stego*) – "to cover, conceal, ward off, resist"
- Always trusts (*pisteuo*) – "to entrust, to commit to one's trust"

- Always hopes (*elpizo*) – "favorable and confident expectation, happy anticipation of good"

- Always perseveres (*hupomeno*) – "to bear up courageously [under suffering]"

- Never fails (*pipto*) – "to fall, loose authority, or cease to have force [sufficient for the need]"

This is quite a list – maybe even a little overwhelming. A personal evaluation (see Appendix A: Love Inventory) of these characteristics can be revealing and serve as a starting point for growth, transformation, and maturity. If you really want an honest evaluation, have your spouse, children, or close colleagues fill it out and give their feedback.

Means to the Goal

The I Timothy 1: 5 Principle has been especially helpful for me because it reveals three personal components that are critical to becoming a loving person: a pure heart, a good conscience, and a sincere faith. Let us look at each of these components.

1. A **pure heart** (*kathros*) is an inner constitution (mind, emotions, and will) that is characterized by a purity that is "free from impure admixture, without blemish, spotless..." This kind of purity comes through the transforming work of the Holy Spirit through the "cleansing... by the washing of water through the word..." (Ephesians 5: 26).

We must learn to allow God to transform us through the "renewing" of our minds (Romans 12: 2). We do this by learning to "take captive every thought to make it obedient to Christ" (II Corinthians 10: 5). Paul states it this way:

> "Finally, brothers, whatever is true, whatever is noble, whatever is right, whatever is pure, whatever is lovely, whatever is admirable – if anything is excellent or praiseworthy – think about such things. Whatever you have learned or received or heard from me – put it into practice. And the God of peace will be with you." (Philippians 4: 8-9, NIV)

Purity of heart is critical for the leader because it is the "pure in heart" that "will see God." (Matthew 5: 8) Purity is the pre-requisite for getting revelation from God. Revelation is essential for our own lives and critical for our leadership. For without vision ("Godly revelation") the people "cast off restraint" (Proverbs 29: 18).

2. A **good conscience** (*agathos*) refers to sensitivity to the conviction of the Holy Spirit so that we can obtain and maintain a conscience that is "good in its character or constitution." It is that ability to be so in touch with God that all of our accounts are clear, above board, above reproach. We are "confessed up" and do not have worry that we will be discovered or exposed by unresolved issues.

There is a difference between condemnation (Romans 8: 1) and conviction. Condemnation is that vague sense that we have done something wrong, or false guilt that plagues the insecure, or the false accusations of the enemy who is "the accuser of our brothers" (Revelation 12: 10).

Conviction is a clear (if we are willing to hear from God) sense that we have violated one or more of God's standards revealed in the Bible. The purpose of conviction is always redemptive and transformational. It is through the confession of our sin that we experience "forgiveness and cleansing" (I John 1: 9). Biblical confession might involve reconciliation or restitution if our sin has hurt others or taken things that belong to them.

We need to prayerfully seek God through the Scriptures and when appropriate wise counsel so that we truly repent of our sin and experience the transformation that is necessary for freedom and effectiveness going forward. Complete confession and repentance is critical in establishing and maintaining a clear conscience. When we do not confess our sin it leads to future vulnerability (see II Corinthians 2: 10-11) to temptation. A good conscience helps us to maintain integrity in life and leadership.

3. A **sincere faith** (*anupokritos*) refers to a faith that is "without hypocrisy." Our lives reflect in attitude and action that which we believe. We are congruent – "what you see is what you get." The author of Hebrews describes faith as "being sure of what we hope for and certain of what we do not see" (11: 1) because we have discovered and have the opportunity to discover again that God is loving, sufficient, and faithful to his promises.

Sincerity of faith is critical for our growth, transformation, and maturity. We must learn that following Christ is not a "formula" but a "faith relationship." We grow from "faith to faith... because the righteous live by faith." (Romans 1: 17, KJV) Without faith we cannot please God.

Why is This Important?

Over the long haul we will become more loving as we cooperate with God in the transformation of our hearts through purity of heart, clarity of conscience, and sincerity of faith. This will lead to greater focus in our sense of God's calling; greater spiritual authority in our service to others; and greater possibilities that we will finish well in our lives and ministries.

The following diagram should help in our understanding of this process of transformation resulting in loving character that manifests itself in Godly focus, spiritual authority, and greater possibilities to finish well in life and ministry.

Diagram 2: The Goal and the Means

I TIMOTHY 1:5

"The goal of this command is love, which comes from a pure heart and a good conscience and a sincere faith."

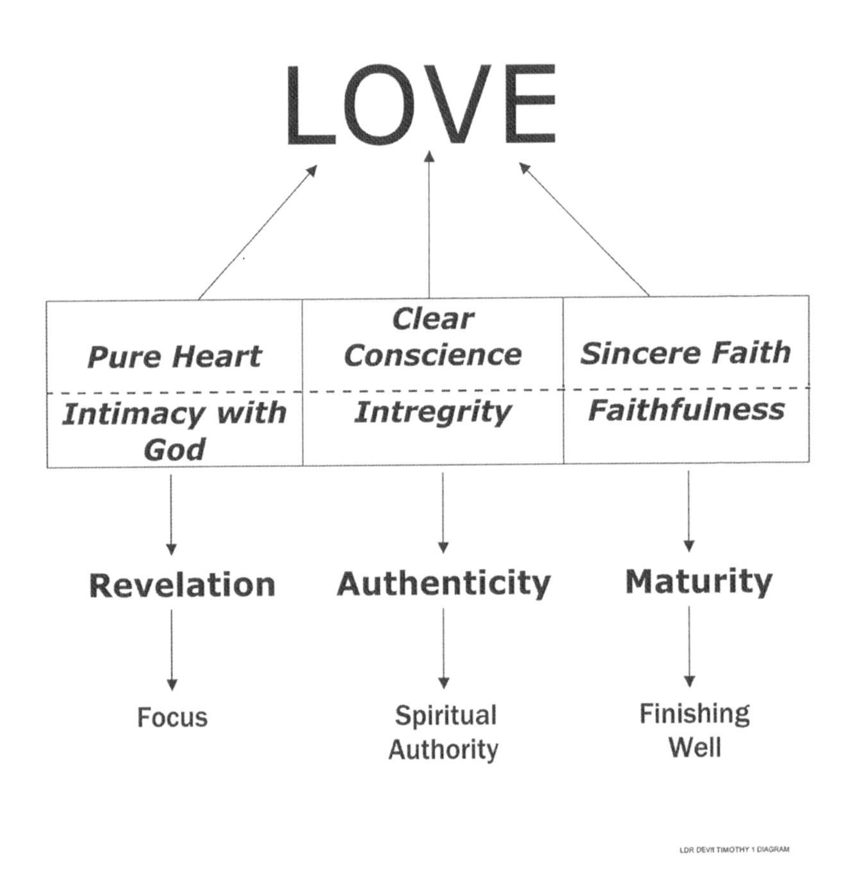

From this diagram, we see that the spiritual formation of purity of heart, clarity of conscience, and sincerity of faith has long-term ramifications that provide a resource base for us to be and act in loving ways.

- Purity of Heart > Intimacy with God > Revelation > Focus
- Clear Conscience > Integrity > Authenticity > Spiritual Authority
- Sincere Faith > Faithfulness > Maturity > Finishing Well

A Firm Foundation

Foundations are the support system that holds up and holds together a structure. Without a solid foundation the structure is at risk. Jesus had some profound words to say about the importance of foundations:

"Therefore everyone who hears these words of mine and puts them into practice is like a wise man who builds his house on the rock. The rain came down, the streams rose, and the winds blew and beat against that house; yet it did not fall, because it had its foundation on the rock. But everyone who hears these words of mine and does not put them into practice is like a foolish man who built his house on sand. The rain came down, the streams rose, and the winds blew and beat against that house, and it fell with a great crash." (Matthew 7: 24-27, NIV) <

Notice that the only difference between the wise and foolish builders was the foundation on which they built. The wise builder built on a foundation of "hearing and practicing," while the foolish builder heard, but did not put the words of Jesus into practice. They both built houses (the foolish builder's house may have been "nicer" than that of the wise builder; we do not know for sure), BUT when the storms of life came, only the wise builder's home remained standing.

Two Types of Hearts

The cultivation of love through a pure heart, good conscience, and a sincere faith will eventually produce a person of passion where the presence and power of God will produce kingdom results in and through their lives and ministries. For those who do not cultivate these qualities they will eventually become fleshly people who experience frustration, futility, and minimal fruit in their lives and ministries.

Those who move toward passion, presence, power, and productivity will be motivated out of grace and submitted to Biblical authority and accountable to others. Those who move toward the flesh, frustration, futility, and failure will be motivated by performance and pragmatism resulting in burnout, blowout, or plateauing. Diagram 3 illustrates this:

Diagram 3: Staying Well

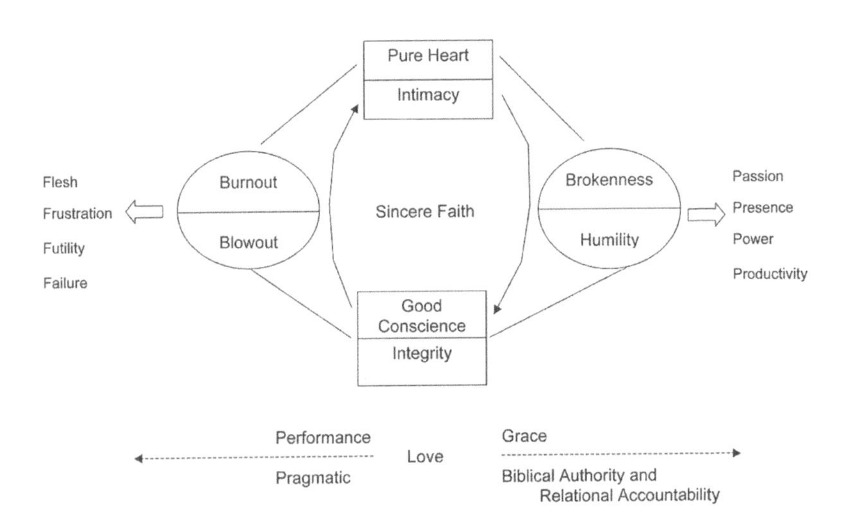

Transformation of our hearts is a process involving a long haul cultivation of relationship with Christ. It is not a formula or self-help program but an "abiding in Christ" resulting in radical transformation over time. For those who learn how to apply The I Timothy 1: 5 Principle in their lives and ministries there is the promise of freedom, fulfillment, and fruitfulness.

Let me illustrate how the I Timothy 1: 5 Principle works out in the lives of a couple of Bible characters. First, let us take a look at a Bible character that did not cultivate this principle over the long haul and ended up burning out, blowing out, and plateauing. You may be surprised at who it is, because he is described in the Bible as having a heart after God (I Samuel 13: 14).

David: Burnout, Blowout, and Plateauing (II Samuel 11-12)

Text: **"In the spring, at the time when kings go off to war... David remained in Jerusalem." (II Samuel 11:1, NIV)**

Background:

- David was one of the 8 sons of Jesse (I Samuel 16:1, 10-12)

- He was a shepherd as a boy (I Samuel 16:11)

- He was anointed as the future king of Israel by Samuel (I Samuel 16:13)

- David was anointed as king of Judah in Hebron (II Samuel 2:4)

- David was crowned king of Israel (II Samuel 5:1-2)

- After David left Hebron, he took more concubines and wives in Jerusalem (II Samuel 5:13, also see Deuteronomy 17:16-17)

- After Jonathan's death there is no record of peer mentoring or relational accountability

Compromise Leading to Burnout, Blowout, and Plateauing:

- David is about 50 years old and has served as king for about 20 years (II Samuel 11)

- David decides not to go to war and stays in Jerusalem (II Samuel 11:1)

- After napping, while on the roof of his palace, he saw a beautiful woman bathing (II Samuel 11:2)

- David sent someone to find out about her/she was Bathsheba, the wife of Uriah (II Samuel 11:3)

- David sent for her and slept with her (II Samuel 11:4)

- Bathsheba become pregnant by David (II Samuel 11:5)

- David tried to cover up his adultery and pregnancy by having Uriah, Bathsheba's husband, return from the battlefield to sleep with her (II Samuel 11: 6-10)

- The cover up does not work as Uriah refuses to sleep with his wife while his countrymen are on the battlefield (II Samuel 11:11-13)

- David ordered Joab, his commander, to murder Uriah by putting him on the front where the strongest defenders were (II Samuel 11:14-15)

- Uriah died in battle (II Samuel 11:17)

- Nathan the prophet confronts David about his sins (II Samuel 12)

- David repents of his sins (Psalms 32 and 51)

- Calamity in David's household results (II Samuel 12:11)/ rebellion of Absalom (II Samuel 15-17)

- The child of adultery dies (II Samuel 12:18) and Solomon is conceived (II Samuel 12:24)

Lessons from David:

- You can have a heart after God and still be vulnerable to burnout, blowout, and plateauing

- David somehow put life on cruise control and neglected the growing cracks in his spiritual formation foundation resulting in vulnerability to sin

- Sin cannot be contained, it must be confessed to be stopped (I John 1:9)

- Sin can be forgiven, but there may be long term consequences (II Samuel 12:11, 18)
- Submitting to God in the consequences can become the context for learning of God's mercy (II Samuel 12:24)
- It is possible to have victory over sin through the power of the Spirit (Romans 6:11-14)
- Intimacy with God is essential for effectiveness in life and ministry (John 15:1-8)

Now, let us look at a Bible character who cultivated the I Timothy 1: 5 Principle over the long haul and through humility and brokenness experienced passion, presence, power, and productivity in his life and ministry.

Caleb: A Man Who Followed God "Wholeheartedly" (Joshua 14: 13-14)

Text: "Then Joshua blessed Caleb son of Jephunneh and gave him Hebron as his inheritance. So Hebron has belonged to Caleb... ever since, because he followed the Lord, the God of Israel, wholeheartedly..."

Background:

- Caleb means "bold, impetuous"
- Caleb is mentioned in only 27 verses in the Bible

- He was a Kenizzite by birth (Numbers 32: 12) and a member of the tribe of Judea (Numbers 13: 6)

- He grew up during the time of captivity in Egypt (Exodus 2: 23-25)

Overview of Caleb's Life:

- Probably one of those who cried out to God for deliverance (Exodus 2: 23-25)

- Experienced hardship in Egypt (Exodus 5)

- Witnessed the return of Moses and the deliverance of Israel out of Egypt (Exodus 7-12)

- Experienced the exodus (Exodus 12: 31-51)

- Witnessed Moses' leadership in the wilderness (Exodus 15: 22-27)

- Witnessed Jethro's visit and counsel to Moses (Exodus 18)

- Witnessed the rebellion at Mt. Sinai (Exodus 32)

- Witnessed the construction/use of tabernacle in the wilderness (Exodus 40)

- Served as one of 12 spies in Canaan (Numbers 13: 6)

- Gave favorable report (along with Joshua) concerning God's ability to give the people the promised land (Numbers 13: 30)

- He was promised Hebron as his inheritance because he followed God wholeheartedly (Deuteronomy 1: 36)

- He wandered in the wilderness for 40 years (Deuteronomy 8: 1-5)

- He witnessed Moses strike the rock instead of speaking to it (Numbers 20: 1-13)

- He witnessed the leadership transition between Moses and Joshua (Deuteronomy 31: 1-8)

- He participated in the conquest of Canaan (Joshua 5-12)

- Caleb received his inheritance and a blessing from Joshua (Joshua 14: 13-14)

- He drove out the Anakites and possessed Hebron (Joshua 15: 14)

- He gave his daughter (Ascah) and her husband (Othniel) the upper/lower springs (Joshua 15: 18)

- Othniel became the first Judge in Israel (Judges 3: 9)

Characteristics of Flowing God Wholeheartedly:

1. Caleb was probably a man of prayer – Exodus 2: 23-25

2. He was promised an inheritance (that he had to fight for) – Exodus 2: 23-25 and Deuteronomy 1: 36

3. He had a long haul perspective and confidence in God's faithfulness – Numbers 13: 30

4. Caleb was a man who persevered until he experienced fulfillment – Joshua 14: 10-12

5. He was patient in God's ways – Joshua 14: 10-12

6. He was passionate ("more vigorous") about God and his purposes – Joshua 14: 10-12

7. Caleb lived a productive life and left a lasting legacy – Joshua 15: 14-17

The focus of this chapter has been on helping you gain an understanding of the importance of establishing, maintaining, and enlarging your spiritual formation foundation (inner-life growth stage and beyond) and how it can affect your life and ministry for good or destruction. The inner-life growth stage is reflected over time in our outward behaviors. If there are inner life problems they will begin to surface as outward behaviors by the time we enter into mid-life.

Understanding and applying the I Timothy 1: 5 Principle is essential to learning how to take care of your inner-life. The quality of transformation in your inner life is the basis (foundation) for you to be and become the person of love that God desires.

If we do not establish, maintain, and enlarge our spiritual formation foundation, we may become vulnerable to burnout, blowout, or plateauing:

* Purity of Heart>Intimacy Cracks>Burnout
* Clarity of Conscience>Integrity Cracks>Blowout
* Sincerity of Faith>Trust Cracks>Plateauing

But how does this work out in the practical day-to-day realities that we live in. Most of us are busy, real busy, and need practical objectives and strategies to integrate concepts like the I Timothy 1: 5 Principle in our lives. In the next three chapters we will take a look at 10 warning signs of burnout, blowout, and plateauing and how we can avoid them as we establish the right kind of foundation for finishing well and leaving a lasting legacy.

Evaluation and Application

1. What's in your toolbox? What are the right tools that you need to be the person God wants you to be so that you can partner with him in his purpose for your life? If you are missing some necessary tools, how do you go about getting them?

2. What is the I Timothy 1: 5 Principle and why is it important? Which side of Diagram 3 are you on? If you are on the left side (moving toward flesh, frustration, futility, failure), how do you get on the right side (moving toward passion, presence, power, productivity)?

3. How did you do on the Love Inventory (Appendix A)? How do you cultivate love in those areas where you are weaker? How do you use love as a primary tool for influencing others?

4. What did you learn from examining and comparing the lives of David and Caleb? Why did one finish well while the other did not? What was the legacy of David and Caleb?

Chapter 4

10 Warning Signs of Burnout

I (Paul) live in the Midwest. During the summer, especially on those hot humid evenings, there are bugs everywhere. While driving through the farm country on back roads you can hit a lot of bugs and really mess up your windshield. The bugs literally explode as they hit, especially the big ones.

Hitting the Windshield

Although this may be a pretty graphic illustration of what burnout looks like, it is actually a pretty realistic picture. When a leader burns out, it usually creates a public mess with profound implications for those in relationship with the leader.

As a former national leader in an association of churches, I saw the effects of leader burnout all too often. The toll on the individual, family, and circle of influence was usually devastating and long lasting. Every time a leader is taken out it causes a ripple effect that is hard to calculate and minimize in terms of collateral damage. It is much better to be pro-active and help leaders avoid burnout than to have to clean up the mess that is caused by hitting the windshield.

What About Bob?

Bob (not his real name) was a successful Christian leader by all external indications. He was well educated, an accomplished athlete, a successful church planter and pastor, a published author, a sought after conference speaker, a husband and father of a large family. He seemed to be thriving in every aspect of his personal and ministry life.

In his early forties he began to have some health problems that were affecting his quality of life and ability to keep up the pace that he had established for himself. He consulted doctors but they were not sure what the source of his health issues were. Some suspected that they might be stress and fatigue related as Bob had been pushing pretty hard for several years without much time off.

His condition worsened and he finally was forced to take a sabbatical of six months to try to figure out his health issues so that he could resume his ministry. It was during this time that I had the opportunity to spend some time with him. We were friends so he asked me for prayer and to give him any insights into his situation that I might have. Over a couple of month period during his sabbatical, I met with Bob several times to listen to him, pray with him, and offer some insights into his situation.

Bob was a classic type A, performance oriented Christian leader. He was a good guy who was extremely talented and gifted, who loved God passionately, and who wanted his life to matter. He had worked hard, made major sacrifices, and had been very successful in life, family, and ministry. He could not figure out what was happening to him.

During our times together I shared with him insights about living and ministering out of a being orientation instead of a doing orientation. We took a look at John 15 and other similar passages and discussed the importance of establishing intimacy with God (along with integrity and faithfulness) as a foundation upon which we build a life and ministry that can lead to finishing well. I shared with him my own story of how I had to re-orient my life and ministry from doing to being in my forties.

Gradually, during Bob's sabbatical, he began to realize that he had become caught up in the momentum of doing good things for God as a basis of his identity and acceptance with God. Gradually, he began to understand that God wanted a relationship with him based on grace, not works. Bob began to understand that his physical condition was (at least in part) related to his performance ("doing") orientation and that if he was going to be able to make it over the long haul he was going to have to make some major changes.

Bob did make several major and necessary changes over time and was able to avoid hitting the windshield of burnout. The primary change that Bob made was to make intimacy with God the foundation of his life and ministry.

What is Burnout?

There are probably some pretty technical definitions for burnout, but I like to think of it in terms of the "inability to continue following God in faithful and fruitful ways because of a lack of intimacy with him." This definition suggests,

1. Inability – we lack resources necessary to face real life/ministry challenges.

2. Following God – our primary relationship and purpose in life.

3. Faithful – we need to cultivate the ability to hear God's voice and obey.

4. Fruitful – we are meant to reproduce "in kind" and leave a legacy for generations to come and for eternity.

BECAUSE OF:

5. Lack of Intimacy – lack of relational connectedness to God resulting in Christ-like transformation in our attitudes and behavior toward others.

Way too many leaders are burning out! But that does not have to happen. If we look to the Bible and the experiences of others who have finished well we can learn to avoid the "intimacy cracks" in our life and ministry foundation that can lead to hitting the windshield of burnout.

Checking Our Foundation for "Intimacy Cracks"

Remember the I Timothy 1: 5 Principle – "The goal of this command is love, which comes from a pure heart and a good conscience and a sincere faith"? The foundation for developing a life and ministry that will transform us into loving people involves establishing a pure heart (the basis for intimacy with God), a good conscience (the basis for integrity), and a sincere faith (the basis for maturity and perseverance).

Over time our inner life is reflected in our outward behaviors. Stress, fatigue, trials, and temptations all put pressure on our inner foundation. Weaknesses in our foundation will eventually be exposed. If there are inner life problems they will begin to surface as outward behaviors by the time we enter into mid-life.

If we do not cultivate ongoing intimacy with God as part of our inner foundation, we will be vulnerable to burnout. Intimacy with God is a source of grace for renewal and transformation so that we can face the challenges of mid-life without having to burn-out. Intimacy ("abiding" in John 15) is a source of supernatural resources that flow through us to conform us to the character of Christ and the purpose of God in us and through us. Remember, "... In all these things [trouble, hardship, persecution, famine, nakedness, danger, sword] we are *more than conquerors* through *him who loved us*." (Romans 8: 37, NIV, italics added)

If this is the case, then why is it so difficult for us to establish intimacy as part of the foundation needed for us to live and lead well as we prepare to finish well? What are the sources (or what I call intimacy cracks) that lead to burnout?

Intimacy Cracks: Sources of Burnout

There are probably as many intimacy cracks as there are people and circumstances. Just about anything can distract me unless I am on guard and determined not to be distracted. But most of us are just trying to survive and do not take the time to develop an ongoing awareness, let alone decide to live pro-actively in terms of establishing and guarding our intimacy with God.

Over the years, I have learned from my own experience and that of others that there are some major intimacy cracks that we need to be aware of and counteract by God's grace if we are to avoid burnout. They include:

1. **Busyness** – life on overload for prolonged periods of time without rest or renewal. Usually associated with an inability to discern what to say "yes" to and what to say "no" to because of performance or pleasing orientation.

2. **Wrong priorities** – life ordered by wrong priorities or inverted priorities. A healthy order of priorities should probably be something like this:

1. God
2. Family
3. Church community
4. Vocation
5. Neighbors
6. Needy

A good way to evaluate your priorities is to see if your calendar and checkbook reflect what you say you value.

3. **Pleasing orientation** – life decisions based on need to please others that usually result in over commitment and a lot of relational drama. We cannot please all the people all the time. A pleasing orientation is usually associated with insecurity that manifests itself in an unhealthy need for the affirmation of others.

4. **Performance orientation** - life decisions based on need to be "successful" which usually leads to over commitment and overload. We are not the Messiah, Jesus is and our role is to abide in him so he can accomplish his purposes in and through us. A performance orientation is usually associated with insecurity that mani-

fests itself in an unhealthy need to gain God's approval through performance.

5. **External demands** – life ordered by the demands of others, crisis, relational drama, health, etc. I call this the survival orientation. We find ourselves so overloaded by life's demands that we tend to shut down and "just do it!" This can be an indication that we are being formed by external circumstances rather than being internally transformed and can lead to burnout.

6. **Dysfunctional relationships** – life ordered by the manipulative agenda of others. Psychologists call this co-dependency. We feel good about ourselves because someone else needs us or we become the rescuer of the weak and needy. There is a legitimate ministry of mercy, but when we create unhealthy dependence on ourselves we may be hindering others from learning healthier ways of relating. Eventually, co-dependent relationships will drain our souls and can lead to resentment, broken relationships, and burnout.

7. **Rejection** – life that is ordered out of an avoidance of potential hurt or lack of forgiveness. Nobody likes to be rejected. It hurts! But in a fallen world people do not always get along and sometimes we hurt one another. Rejection seems to be part of life. When we are affected by rejection in unhealthy ways we can be overly careful about entering into relationships, judge others through the grid of past relationships, and become embittered because we have not forgiven. Rejection may happen, but we do not have to be defined by it. We can learn from it, forgive, and learn to love (even our enemies).

These intimacy cracks can produce weaknesses in our foundation that can lead to burnout. Weaknesses in our foundation, if not repaired, can lead to major breakdowns as the pressures of life and responsibilities mount. Since we all are in process, how can we know if our inner foundation is strong enough to hold up when the weight of life, leadership, and ministry are increased?

Over time, if we have not cultivated intimacy with God as part of the foundation of our inner life our intimacy cracks will begin to demonstrate specific types of behavior that can serve as warning signs of potential burnout.

10 Warning Signs of Burnout

The following list of warning signs is based on my experience and observations from working with leaders over the years. This list is not inspired or all encompassing. It is practical and meant to serve as a means to help us evaluate ourselves before we hit the windshield and splat all over the place. Prayerfully consider the following warning signs and let the Holy Spirit "lead you into all truth" in this matter. For further application, I have provided a self-evaluation form in Appendix B: Burnout Inventory. Warning signs for potential burnout may include:

1. Inconsistent devotional life (loss of sense of the presence and peace of God).

This is a difficult area for many (especially if you are a type A personality – task oriented). Many of the models for quiet times work for some but not for everyone. The same time, same way formula may be a good place to start, but can become boring and legalistic. But a consistent devotional life is absolutely critical if we are to mature as disciples and have the necessary perspective and power to avoid burnout.

There are many resources available that can help us in this area, but we have to find our own way. We cannot wear Saul's armor (I Samuel 17: 38-40). We need to find what works for us. I will share briefly my own experience in Chapter 7: Establishing Disciplines of Faithfulness. Basic to my experience are realities of grace, relationship, and peace. I need to maintain a renewing (and transforming) balance of these three realities in my life if I am going to avoid burnout.

When I am not "abiding" regularly with God I begin to loose my sense of God's presence, power, and peace. When this happens I need to take the time and make the adjustments needed to regain right relationship with God. The danger here is that I can neglect my regular connecting with God and live on the edges of intimacy. This is a dangerous place to be and can easily lead to rationalization that can lead to big trouble. Honesty, accountability, and planned periodic times of retreat can help keep me from living too close to the edges.

I like the way Dietrich Bonhoeffer (*Christ the Center*) describes this potential danger. He says that we need to live with Christ as the center of our lives not as the "God of the gaps." If relationship with Christ is central to every aspect of our lives and ministries, then we have a better chance of staying connected to him and his purposes.

2. Inability to manage daily schedule (regularly working more than 8 hour days).

Busy people have busy schedules and those schedules can get out of control at times. It is easy to schedule tight and have very little room for the unplanned crises that inevitably come. Many of us have major responsibilities in our lives. We work hard and try to work smart, but sometimes it seems that the work never really gets done.

I have learned to prayerfully attempt to manage my schedule, allowing for times of reflection and crisis management. I intentionally build margins into my schedule and also evaluate my schedule based on my core values and priorities to make sure that my schedule reflects these values and priorities.

Those of us who tend to be people pleasers or performance oriented are especially vulnerable here. We can tend to say yes too often and can get overcommitted. We can over promise and under deliver, which will eventually hinder our credibility. Over time, over commitment can lead to longer and longer days and less and less time for family, recreation, and other activities that we need to keep ourselves balanced and healthy.

3. Inconsistent day off (at least once per week).

There are times when you just have to "get 'er done," even if it means working long hours or on your day off. Leadership and ministry is like that, it is not an "8-5" deal with over-time wages for anything over 40 hours. It seems like we are never really off. We get phone calls at dinner, crisis calls late at night or early in the morning. It never seems to stop and then there are the really bad days.

Because of the ambiguous nature of leadership, we must learn to manage our schedules, develop others to help, and train our people to know when it is appropriate to contact us and when it is not. If we do not, we will eventually become so stressed and stretched that we will quit or burn out.

Remember Moses (Exodus 18) and the Apostles (Acts 6) when they were overwhelmed with the demands of the people in their charge. In both cases they managed their schedules by delegating to others to help so that they could focus on what they were called to do and remain sane in the process.

If we cannot make room in our schedules for regular days off, we are probably being managed by our schedules and other peoples expectations rather than being balanced and healthy. Inadequate time for family, reflection, or recreation can deplete our resources and set us up for burnout.

4. Lack of recreational interests and regular exercise (2-3 times per week).

When there are so many needs all around us it can be a little guilt producing to take off early and go play golf with a friend (or tennis in my case). It can also be a little guilt producing when you go to pay for the ground's fees (or the indoor tennis court fees). "What will others think?" "Am I being a good steward?" "Shouldn't I being using this money and time to serve really needy people?" Really good questions, but they need to be balanced with the reality that reasonable recreational activities may be needed to keep us from burning out.

As I have gotten older, I have discovered that I cannot be intense all the time. I just do not have it in me any longer. That does not mean that I have become cynical and a slacker. No, I just need to pace myself more if I am going to make it to the finish line.

Along the way I have begun to recognize the enjoyment (and renewal) of other things besides work! We all will have to work the details of this out in our own context, but I am convinced that regular recreation and exercise can lead to a more balanced, enjoyable, and healthy life.

Without some healthy escapes we can get trapped in the intensity of our life and leadership demands in ways that can be crushing and lead to burnout. Recreation can be an opportunity for rest and renewal (and a lot of fun and fellowship). Without it, the load of life can be pretty heavy and even crushing.

5. Frequent fatigue, discouragement, and depression (prone to sickness).

By the time we enter into mid-life our life choices begin to catch up with us. The foundation that we laid will either be able to hold up to the weight of life and leadership demands or the intimacy cracks will begin to weaken our foundations and cause partial and even complete cave-ins. In mid-life we may discover that we are running on fumes unless we have established regular fueling strategies.

Remember Bob. That is what happened to him. He was exceptional is so many areas, but life's demands and pressures caught up to him and he began to have health problems. Later in this chapter we will take a look at Elijah and see how he crashed and burned after his amazing victory over the prophets of Baal on Mount Carmel.

Not all physical and mental health problems are caused by stress, but some may be. If we are struggling in these areas, we need to consult the best doctors and mental health professionals available. But we may also want to ask God for insight into our condition. Please do not misunderstand me; I know this is a tricky area. What I am saying is that we need discernment to know if our condition is physical, psychological, or spiritual.

I believe that some health issues can be (at least in part) related to prolonged stress and over work. If this is the case, we need to make necessary changes to put ourselves in the place of balance and health. If we do not we will more than likely hit the windshield of burnout.

6. Lack of enjoyment in life, leadership, and ministry (frequent thoughts of quitting).

Over time, we can get caught in the gears of life and leadership. It can seem like we never do enough to keep up, or do enough to keep people happy, or do enough to keep out of crisis. For many conscientious leaders the solution for challenges like these has been to work harder and smarter. There are times when this strategy is necessary and effective, but for the long haul it may lead to a lack of fulfillment and discouragement.

The bottom line is that over the long haul, hard work, even smart work, will not be enough. If we have not cultivated an "abiding" relationship of intimate connectedness with God, we will not have the perspective and power to press through the impossible into God's possible. We will get tired, discouraged, and may even quit.

So many times in my earlier years I quit just before the break through because I was relying on my own strength, my own ability, my own gifts, and my own sense of purpose. We need the resources of God to do his will. Through intimate connection with God we can gain a godly perspective and learn of the supernatural resources available for his people to accomplish his will. Apart from this intimate connection with God we will tend to rely on our own resources and sooner or later hit the windshield of burnout.

God's purposes take God's resources to accomplish. Without them we will not enjoy life and leadership to the level that he intends and will loose heart that can lead to shutting down or quitting. In life and leadership there will be difficult seasons, but there can be joy in the journey (John 16: 33). If we are discouraged and want to quit, we may want to make sure that we are intimately connected to God who is the source of joy and fruitfulness.

7. Frequent friction with spouse and children (easily frustrated and angry).

The responsibilities and burdens of life and leadership can take a toll on our families and us. We can find ourselves so depleted from stress and over work that we have little emotional energy left for our spouse and children.

Different personalities process this dynamic in different ways. If we are introverted we may shut down and disengage relationally. We become aloof and distant. We may be there physically but not there emotionally. This can cause major marital and family problems, as healthy communication is critical for the well being of family members. Lack of healthy communication can lead to misunderstandings, insecurity, resentment, and displays of anger.

For the extravert, communication can become self-centered where there is not healthy give and take. Listening to the problems of significant others without problem solving or reciprocal listening can get pretty old. Extraverts also tend to tell it like they see or feel it and can say things that are not true, appropriate, or helpful. "All give and no get" can lead to break down of communication, frustration, and anger.

We need to have enough left in our emotional tanks for our spouses and children. When we drag home dead tired again and again and do not have anything left for the most important people in our lives there is something wrong. Over time we may loose relational connection with the ones we love and need most. In this life, if you do not have a relatively healthy marriage and family, you do not have much.

Most marriages and families have rough times when communication is difficult. But if we use work and leadership as a means for personal fulfillment or as an escape from the challenges of growing in our marriages and family, we will eventually find ourselves in jeopardy of loosing them.

8. Frequent friction with boss and staff/ co-workers (easily impatient and judgmental).

Just as with our spouses and children, the long haul effects of inadequate connectedness with God will affect our relationships with bosses, staff, or co-workers. Love (remember I Timothy 1: 5) is the necessary resource for healthy relationships. Without love we may not be able to properly submit to authority, be patient with others, confront issues in others effectively, or build healthy and effective teams.

We may experience some of the same types of personality patterns in our work place as we do at home, although we may be able to fake it easier and longer at work. How we handle "no" in our lives may be especially revealing in the work place. It is pretty easy to get along as long as we get our way. When we are confronted with obstacles to getting our way, it may reveal our hearts. If we have not cultivated an intimate connection with God we will tend to rely on fleshly resources rather than love.

We may tend to become impatient with others and blame or judge them for our frustrations. We may become manipulative or loose our temper. Either way, we will pay a price in the long haul for our lack of love. Patterns of aggression and passive aggression may be indications that we are not relying on God, but our flesh, leading to frustration, lack of fulfillment, ineffectiveness, and possible burnout.

9. Growing number of uncompleted tasks, projects (missed appointments and unfulfilled commitments).

In some cases we can become so overwhelmed with our life responsibilities and pressures that we cannot any longer hold it together. We begin to forget meetings, get behind schedule, and fail to meet objectives. Some of us are just unorganized and struggle with our schedules as a natural course. But effective leadership involves at least a basic sense of order and follow through.

I know that I am nearing overload when I cannot find necessary information in my unique filing system. I am pretty good at multitasking, but tend to take on more than I have time for. Also, I am pretty good on the idea, implementation stages, but pretty useless on the development, maintenance stages of program development. Knowing our strengths and weaknesses can help in managing our schedule, but if we commit to something we need to see it through or we risk loosing credibility.

Keeping appointments is especially important because they are relational. Being on time or calling ahead if we will be delayed sends a message of value to the person we are meeting with. How we treat the little people is especially revealing in this matter. Do we show up on time for the big shots and blow off the little guys? We need to be careful here because there are no little people in the kingdom. Loosing control of our schedules and devaluing people can be an indication that we have intimacy cracks in our foundation that can lead to burnout.

10. Disconnection relationally with mentor(s) (lack of accountability).

If we try to live our lives apart from intimate connection with God we will probably develop a denial system that resists the conviction of the Holy Spirit. We will rationalize our choices and sanctify our "sacrificial" life style. We will also tend to surround ourselves with yes people and keep our distance from those who may tell us the truth in love.

Busyness makes it easier for us to not include mentors and accountable relationships in our lives. Because we all have blinders, we may be headed for the windshield and not know it. We need healthy and effective people in our lives to help us see our weaknesses, point out possible problems, and help us be more effective people and leaders. Without mentors and accountability in our lives we are like bugs flying head long into the windshields of freeway traffic. We may not hit the first few windshields, but sooner or later watch out!

Because accountability and mentoring are so important for finishing well and establishing a lasting legacy, Chapter 10: Accountability and Mentoring will cover this topic is greater detail. Before turning to our Biblical example of blowout, take a break and prayerfully do the self-evaluation found in Appendix B: Burnout Inventory.

Now, let's take a look at the Old Testament prophet Elijah and see what we can learn from his experience of hitting the windshield of burnout and recovering to tell us about it. Let's take a look at his life and see what we can learn from his experience.

Elijah: Burnout and Restoration (I Kings 19)

Text: "Elijah was afraid and ran for his life. When he came to Beersheba in Judah, he left his servant there, while he himself went a day's journey into the desert. He came to a broom tree, sat down under it and prayed that he might die. 'I have had enough, Lord,' he said. 'Take my life; I am no better than my ancestors.' Then he lay down under the tree and fell asleep." (I Kings 19: 3-5, NIV)

Context: Elijah had just defeated the prophets of Baal on Mount Carmel (I Kings 18) but was now a fugitive being pursued by Queen Jezebel (I Kings 19: 1-2)

Overview of the Life and Ministry of the Prophet Elijah – "my God is Yahweh [God as covenant keeper]"

- Elijah, the Tishbite, ministered during the reign of King Ahab and Queen Jezebel (I Kings 17:1)

- Elijah prophesied "neither dew nor rain" for 3 ½ years (I Kings 17:2, James 5:17)

- Elijah hid in the Kerith Ravine where he is provided food by ravens (I Kings 17:3-6) until the brook dries up (I Kings 17:7)

- Elijah went to Zarephath of Sidon where he staid with a widow and God multiplies the flour and oil for making bread (I Kings 17:7-16)
- Elijah raised the widow's son from the dead (I Kings 17:17-24)
- Elijah confronted Ahab about "abandoning the Lord's commands" and "following the Baals" (I Kings 18:18)
- Elijah confronted the prophets of Baal on Mount Carmel and the fire of God fell on the flooded alter that Elijah had prepared (I Kings 18:19-38)
- The people repented and the prophets of Baal were killed (I Kings 18:39-40)
- Elijah prophesied the end of the draught and raced on foot before Ahab in his chariot as he returned to Jezreel (I Kings 18:41-46)
- Jezebel tried to kill Elijah and he fled into the wilderness out of fear (I Kings 19:1-3)
- Elijah is renewed by God as he ate, slept, and heard the "gentle whisper" of God (I Kings 19:4-13)
- God revealed to Elijah that he is not "the only one left" but that there were 7,000 who have not bowed down to the Baals (I Kings 19:14-18)
- Elijah called Elisha to become his attendant (I Kings 19:19-21)

- Elijah confronted Ahab about the murder of Naboth and the theft of his vineyard (I Kings 21:17-19)

- Ahab was killed during the battle at Ramoth Gilead in fulfillment of Elijah's prophecy (I Kings 22:37-38)

- Elijah called down fire on two captain and their 50 men (I Kings 1:9-12)

- Elijah prophesied the death of King Ahaziah (II Kings 1:15-17)

- Elijah called Elisha to be his understudy (I Kings 19: 19-21)

- Elisha asked for a "double portion" of Elijah's spirit (II Kings 2:9)

- Elisha followed Elijah across the Jordon River where Elijah was taken to heaven in a chariot of fire (II Kings 2:11)

- Elisha saw this, cried out "my father, my father," and picked up Elijah's fallen cloak (II Kings 2:12-13)

- Elisha walked back to the Jordon and used the cloak to part the waters (II Kings 2:14)

- John the Baptist is compared to Elijah (Matthew 11:14, 16:14, 17:10-12, Mark 9:12-13, Luke 1:17, John 1:21-25)

- Elijah appeared with Moses on the Mount of Transfiguration (Matthew 17:3-4, Mark 9:4, Luke 9:30)

- Elijah is possibly one of the two end-time witnesses (Revelation 11:3)

Lessons from the Life of Elijah:

1. Prolonged and difficult life and leadership challenges can take a toll on us emotionally, spiritually, and/or physically.

2. After great victories a leader may be vulnerable to doubts, discouragement, or depression.

3. In a depleted condition, leaders may be unusually vulnerable to emotions (i.e. fear) and want to quit (i.e. run from their situations).

4. In times of doubt, discouragement, and depression a leader wants to make sure he/she is eating well, getting enough sleep, and taking times for refreshing.

5. An intimate encounter with God is necessary for renewal and refocus.

6. Learn from the experiences of the past so that we do not have to repeat them.

7. Follow God and invest in the next generation.

In this chapter we have taken a look at burnout and the example of the Old Testament Prophet Elijah. We have described the importance of cultivating intimacy with God, how intimacy cracks develop, and ten warning signs of burnout. In the next chapter we will describe blowout, integrity cracks, and the 10 warning signs of blowout.

Evaluation and Application

1. What is the definition of burnout? Why is establishing, maintaining, and enlarging our foundation of intimacy important for navigating the challenges of mid-life if we want to finish well? How would you rate your devotional life? What areas do you need to improve and how are you going to go about it?

2. What intimacy cracks did you discover in your foundation? If you have any, how are you going to repair them?

3. How did you do on the Burnout Inventory? What are the specific area(s) that you are vulnerable? How are you going to strengthen these areas and guard yourself from becoming more vulnerable to burnout?

4. What did you learn from studying the life of Elijah? What lessons do you need to apply to your own life and how do you plan to do so?

Chapter 5

10 Warning Signs of Blowout

Moral failure is all too prevalent in church leaders today with devastating consequences! I have seen so many good leaders go down for the count because of moral compromise. Remember David and Bathsheba? It just took one look (and an invitation) to really mess up a good thing resulting in tragic consequences! But, as we learned earlier, David's immoral act began in his heart long before he finally acted it out (see Chapter 2, "David: burnout and blowout"). Remember, we "nibble ourselves lost!"

Just One Look (That's All it Took)!

The following story is a compilation of several real life situations that will illustrate how little compromises become big problems. Bill (not his real name) was a successful pastor of a growing church in a suburban community. He was a bit of a workaholic, but he was very devoted to his family and ministry. He tried to be there for his wife and children while meeting the demands of a growing ministry.

Bill was very careful to conduct his ministry in ways that were professional and "above reproach." He had specific guidelines for male-female interaction and even had an accountability partner. He had regular quiet times with God and studied the Bible regularly for sermon preparation and personal growth.

Over time, the demands on Bill began to pull him in many directions. The church had grown large enough to support a secretary and youth pastor, but managing them along with all the other duties and responsibilities that he had was stretching him thin. With the addition of more people in the church and on staff, there seemed to be more problems, challenges, and outright crises.

Bill began to cut back on his regular quiet time and was not able to give as much time to Bible study. He was finding it more difficult to maintain a relationship with his accountability partner. It seemed like he was going from meeting to meeting and from crisis to crisis. He began to feel like he was trying to juggle with his hands tied behind his back or herd cats. But Bill kept telling himself that this was just a season and that everything would settle down once ... (you fill in the blank here).

Bill's personal moral crisis began while he was attending a conference on breaking the 250-barrier. He had looked forward to this time away as a mini-retreat, a time to relax and let down while learning some needed information about what his church was currently dealing with. The first evening of the conference after the introductory session, Bill returned to his hotel room and turned on the TV to catch the sports on ESPN.

As he channel surfed, his eyes caught an "adult situation" that was being shown on a cable channel. In shock he quickly clicked to the next channel, but he also found himself aroused. Over the next several minutes he battled with his arousal and his desire to be pure. But in his mind he was wrestling. After all, it was not pornography, only an adult situation. He clicked back to the channel, more out of curiosity than evil intend. After all, it is only sex. What's the big deal?

That night a seed was planted. Bill began to have sexual thoughts and even checked out some adult sites on his personal computer late at night after his wife and children had gone to bed. He had told them that he needed to work on church business and that he would be done in a little while. His wife trusted him and knew that he was working hard and sometimes needed to do a little extra work at night after the kids were in bed.

As Bill's curiosity began to take hold of him he felt guilty and trapped. He knew that what he was doing was wrong and confessed his sin again and again. But he could not seem to break free from this secret sin. He could not tell anybody what was going on for fear of what they might think or that he might loose his job. He was so ashamed, but thought that he could handle his problem.

Bill did not get to this place all at once. Little things began to mount up into a big mess and he felt trapped. The rest of the story is not pretty. Eventually Bill was found out and his life and ministry were dramatically and shamefully affected. Sooner or later all "Bills" are found out.

This pattern continued until one day his church board confronted Bill. It seems that Bill had carelessly accessed pornography on his church office computer and it had come to the attention of his board.

Bill had failed to maintain regular intimacy with God that led to the compromise of his integrity. He had not consistently applied the I Timothy 1: 5 Principle and had not maintained a pure heart (intimacy), a clear conscience (integrity), and a sincere faith (maturity and perseverance). This eventually resulted in blowout. Bill repented, was forgiven, and could eventually be restored; but at what cost?

Integrity cracks in the foundation of our lives and leadership will eventually be revealed or exploited resulting in blowout and all the horrible ramifications of guilt, shame, hurt, hypocrisy, disgrace, and failure. It is not pretty and it can be avoided. Far too many leaders fall into the trap that Bill fell into. There are no little or unseen sins. We must learn to deal with sin before it takes hold and destroys our lives and those we love and serve.

What is Blowout?

Again, there are probably some pretty technical definitions for blowout, but I like to think of it in terms of the "inability to continue following God in faithful and fruitful ways because of a lack of integrity with him and others." This definition suggests,

1. Inability – we lack resources necessary to face real life/ministry challenges.

2. Following God – our primary relationship and purpose in life.

3. Faithful – we need to cultivate the ability to hear God's voice and obey.

4. Fruitful – we are meant to reproduce "in kind" and leave a legacy for generations to come and for eternity.

BECAUSE OF:

5. Lack of Integrity – lack of moral connectedness to God him resulting in Christ-like transformation in our attitudes and behavior toward others.

In most cases of blowout there is probably a breach in intimacy with God as well. When we become over worked and fatigued we tend to be more vulnerable to integrity issues and moral compromise.

Again, way too many leaders are blowing out. But we do not have to. We can learn from David and the "Bills" around us and by the grace of God learn how to live and lead well so that we can finish well and leave a lasting legacy.

Checking Our Foundation for "Integrity Cracks"

I use the human pyramid exercise to illustrate the importance of a strong foundation in my teaching to younger emerging leaders on starting well. I have them break up into teams and see who can build the highest human pyramid. Once they complete their pyramid and are safely re-seated, I ask them about their design and strategy for building the winning pyramid.

They tell me that it is about the foundation. If you do not get the foundation right, the pyramid will not be able to stand up to increased weight over time as they add the layers. They also tell me that the break down of the pyramid happens at the weakest points. The weight of the structure seems to attack the weakest place.

And so it is with our lives! If we want a life and ministry that will stand up over the long haul and through the challenges of mid-life, we must build, maintain, and enlarge a solid foundation. Jesus described this reality in his teaching on the wise and foolish builders (Matthew 7: 24-27):

> "Therefore everyone who hears these words of mine and *puts them into practice* is like a wise man who built his house on the rock. The rain came down, the streams rose, and the winds blew and beat against that house; yet it did not fall, because it had its foundation on the rock. But everyone who hears these words of mine and *does not put them into practice* is like a foolish man who

> built his house on sand. The rain came down, the streams rose and the winds blew and beat against that house, and it fell with a great crash." (NIV, *parenthesis mine*)

Note here that the only difference between the house that fell and the one that did not was obedience to the words of Jesus. Integrity is "practicing" Jesus' teaching; and lack of integrity is not "practicing" his teaching.

If we want to be able to withstand the challenges of life and leadership we have to make sure that we are examining our foundations for integrity cracks and learn to practice the teaching of Jesus until our foundation is rock solid.

Integrity Cracks: Sources of Blowout

There are many sources of moral compromise that results in integrity cracks. A look at a passage like Galatians 5: 19-21 is a good place to begin. Paul says that "the acts of the sinful nature are obvious" and then gives the following list:

- sexual immorality
- impurity
- debauchery
- idolatry
- witchcraft
- hatred
- discord

- jealousy
- fits of rage
- selfish ambition
- dissensions
- factions
- envy
- drunkenness
- orgies
- and the like (suggesting that there are more)

This is quite a list (and there are several other similar lists in the Bible that reveal the depravity of our sinful humanity). It is not a pretty sight, but there is hope! Right after Paul lists the "acts of the sinful nature," he describes the "fruit of the Spirit" which is the inheritance of all true believers who learn to practice the teaching of Jesus through the power of the Holy Spirit. Paul says, "the fruit of the Spirit is love, joy, peace, patience, kindness, goodness, faithfulness, gentleness and self-control" (Galatians 5: 22-23, NIV).

What a contrast! And what a hope! It's good to know that there is an alternative, but we have to diligently establish and maintain this hope if we are to live and lead well. Over the years, I have learned from my own experience and that of others that there are some major integrity cracks that we need to be aware of and counteract by God's grace if we are to avoid blowout. They include:

1. **Selfishness** – a life centered on a "me and mine" orientation where what is best for me is always the bottom line. Selfishness can be very subtle in its manifestations. It is very easy to confuse wants

and needs. We can easily develop a life orientation where self-fulfillment or self-actualization is a primary goal and motivation.

The Bible promises us that God will meet our needs as we seek him first in our lives (Matthew 6: 33). Our culture promises us that our needs will be met through "making it happen" or "taking care of number one." We all struggle with selfishness, but unless we learn to die to our self we will never experience the freedom, fulfillment, and fruitfulness that God wants for his people (John 12: 24).

2. **Identity issues** – a life and ministry can be greatly influenced by a faulty sense of identity. Most of us struggle at times with a sense of inadequacy. This can manifest itself in one of two extremes: inferiority or superiority. Both of these expressions of identity can lead to dysfunction and destruction.

The Bible describes the believer's identity as that of a "new creation" where old things have passed away and new things are being established (II Corinthians 5: 17). Key to this new creation identity is the reality that our resources alone no longer define us, but we now have the resources of Christ to overcome our selfishness and become like him (Philippians 4: 13).

3. **Sexual immorality** – all humans are sexual by nature. Our sexuality is complex and affected by our family, our culture, and our life style choices. Sexual immorality is the misuse of the gift of sexuality that God has given us. Sexuality must be established in purity if it is to be expressed and enjoyed in the healthy ways that God intends (Titus 1: 15-16).

The establishing of purity in our lives involves winning the battle of the mind (II Corinthians 10: 3-5) where we learn to break the power of lust (Matthew 5: 27-30) that can lead to immoral behavior. If we do not learn to "bring *every* thought captive to Christ" we may become vulnerable to a raunchy thought life that can eventually lead to pornography and acting out in sexually immoral ways.

4. **Ambition** – a life and ministry that is based on "selfish ambition" may look good on the outside (at least for awhile) but is fleshly on the inside. Although there is a legitimate type of ambition (I Timothy 3: 1), Jesus called the teachers of the law and the Pharisees

of his day "white washed" tombs (Matthew 23: 27) because in their ambition to be righteous they had become legalistic. They looked good on the outside but were like "dead men's bones" and "full of greed and self-indulgence" (Matthew 23: 25) on the inside. But sooner or later, what is on the inside is exposed. If our ambition is self-centered it will eventually produce the fruit of the flesh.

5. **Greed** – a life and ministry that is based on "what's in it for me" as opposed to service out of obedience. Greed can be subtle, especially in a materialistic culture that confuses success with wealth and power. The Bible teaches that a "worker deserves his wages" (I Timothy 5: 18) but also that "godliness with contentment is great gain" (I Timothy 6: 6). Paul warns that, "people who want to get rich fall into temptation and a trap and into many foolish and harmful desires that plunge men into ruin and destruction." (I Timothy 6: 9) Greed can lead to compromise and a pragmatic approach to life and leadership that leads to hypocrisy and destruction.

6. **Incongruity** – a life and ministry that is not true to a Biblical core of values even though it might give lip service to these values. Incongruity is usually revealed when the pressure is on, when it may cost us some thing to remain committed to our stated core values.

The Bible describes incongruity in several ways. We mentioned the hypocrisy of the teachers of the law and the Pharisees above. Another insightful description is that of being "double-minded" (James 1: 8). Double-mindedness or "conflicting desires" leads to instability. In another passage, Jesus says, "no one can serve two masters" (Matthew 6: 24). Sooner or later one master or set of values will take over. Our core values will be tested and we must remain consistent to them if we want to live and lead in a way that honors God and positively impacts others.

7. **Rationalization** – the ability to make us look good or justify our actions when we have blown it or done something wrong. We all have the tendency to rationalize and justify ourselves. Deceit is part of our fallen nature (Romans 1: 29) and we are vulnerable to the lies and accusations of the enemy (John 8: 44), the world

(II Corinthians 4: 4), and others (Matthew 24: 4). This is why we need to be people who live according to the clear teachings of the Bible, are led by the Holy Spirit, and accountable to others. We all have blind spots that if not dealt with can cause us to make costly mistakes or lead us into sin that will devastate us, our families, and those we serve and influence.

These integrity cracks can produce weaknesses in our foundation that can lead to blowout. Weaknesses in our foundation, if not strengthen or repaired, can lead to major breakdowns as the pressures of life and responsibilities of leadership mount. Since we all are in process, how can we know if our inner foundation is strong enough to hold up when the weight of life and leadership are increased?

Over time, if we have not cultivated integrity as part of the foundation of our inner life and have given in to compromise, we will begin to demonstrate specific types of behavior that can serve as warning signs of potential blowout.

10 Warning Signs of Blowout

The following list of warning signs is based on my experience and observations from working with leaders over the years. It is not inspired or all encompassing. It is practical and meant to serve as a means to help us evaluate ourselves so that we can take corrective measures before we crash and burn. Prayerfully consider the following warning signs and let the Holy Spirit "lead you into all truth" in this matter. Warning signs for potential blowout may include:

1. Secret life involving fantasy and behavior (eventually leading to bondage).

Very few people wake up one morning and decide to make decisions that will ruin their lives, destroy their families, and cause major damage to people who they are invested in. Usually blowouts are caused by small cracks that become major ones from being pressured over time. Small cracks can eventually lead to major compromises in our foundation leading to blowout.

These cracks in our foundation begin little and grow gradually over time. The fact that we do not get caught or busted for private thoughts or actions does not mean that we are getting away with it. The fact that we are not immediately judged for private sin (or any other type of sin) is because of God's mercy. He is giving us time to repent. It is his mercy (or "kindness") that "triumphs over judgment" (James 2: 13).

As leaders we need to set a righteous standard for our thought life and behavior that is "above reproach" (I Timothy 3: 2.) We must be uncompromising with sin and not give it an opportunity to fester and grow. Sin is like cancer, it may start small but if it is not destroyed it will grow and eventually kill us!

Like Bill, pornography is a major temptation for many men (and women) in today's permissive hypersexual culture. We must be careful about what we watch, read, and listen to. We need to be accountable to others, set up guidelines, and Internet blocks on our computers. We must do whatever it takes to stay as far away from sexual (and other) temptations as possible. This is not some sort of retreat from the world, but an attempt to defeat worldliness before we are compromised and become entrapped!

2. Justification of behaviors as personal "rights or liberties" (at the expense of living a life above reproach).

In order to live with the tensions of a secret life we tend to rationalize and justify our behaviors, first of all to ourselves and then later to others. We tend to be very hard on others who are involved in similar types of behavior. The Bible describes this as the "splinter and beam syndrome" (Matthew 7: 1-5). We tend to project our sin on others in judgment and justify our behavior as "not that bad" or "under control."

Another common form of justification is the appeal to personal rights and freedoms. After all, it was for freedom that we were redeemed. The law kills, but grace leads to freedom! "All people sin." "We are all weak in our humanity." "Life is meant to be enjoyed." "I deserve a little indulgence after all I have sacrificed." Arguments like this can sound so right, but in the end they "lead to death" (Proverbs 14: 12).

If challenged by others about our rationalization, we may distance ourselves from them. We may fall into the trap of hiding behind the "God's anointed" argument or the "who are you to judge" argument and begin to surround ourselves with yes people. This is very dangerous territory and can lead to a deception that ultimately can isolate leaders from needed accountability, support, and help. Over time leaders who justify sin in their lives will be revealed for who they really are and their lives and ministries will be discredited.

3. Inconsistent devotional life (loss of sense of presence and peace of God).

I have already commented on this in the previous chapter. This characteristic is common to all three of the outcomes of failing to apply the I Timothy 1: 5 Principle. Let me repeat that this is a difficult area for many (especially if you are a type A personality – task oriented). Many of the models for quiet times work for some but not for everyone. The same time, same way formula may be a good place to start but can become boring and legalistic. But a consistent devotional life is absolutely critical if we are to mature as disciples and have the necessary perspective and power to avoid blowout.

4. Lack of accountable relationships (unwilling to be teachable and surrounding yourself with "yes" people).

I have already commented on this as well in the previous chapter and will address it is more detail in Chapter 11: Accountability and Mentoring. Briefly, if we try to live our lives apart from intimate connection with God we will probably develop a denial system that resists the conviction of the Holy Spirit while distancing ourselves from healthy accountability.

Justification of sin makes it hard for us to include mentors and accountability relationships in our lives. We need healthy and honest people in our lives to help us see our weaknesses, point out possible problems, and help us be more authentic people and effective leaders. Without mentors and accountability in our lives we are vulnerable. Remember, "Iron sharpens iron, so one man sharpens another" (Proverbs 27: 17).

We need to remain teachable and invite trusted others into our lives to help us stay sharp and focused. We all need a Nathan (II Samuel 12) in our lives, even if we do not like his message. It is better to be confronted about sin early on before it begins to get a death hold on us and destroys the work of God in and through us.

5. Insistence of having your own way (dogmatic, argumentative, unwilling to compromise on "non-essentials").

As we become more and more unwilling to learn from others, we will tend to become dogmatic, argumentative, and unwilling to compromise. We have found the formula or have arrived so it is "our way or the highway!"

Those who challenge us or ask for details are a hindrance that we need to get rid of. As leaders, we demand followers who will submit. God has given us a vision and followers need to "get on board or get out of the way!"

This type of leadership can appear to be strong leadership, but it can also become abusive. Ken Blue (*Healing Spiritual Abuse*) describes seven characteristics of abusive leaders from Matthew 23. He states that abusive leaders:

1. Base their spiritual authority on their position or office rather than on their service to the group;

2. Often say one thing but do another;

3. Manipulate people by making them feel guilty or not measuring up spiritually;

4. Are preoccupied with looking good and keeping up appearances;

5. Seek honorific titles and special privileges that elevate them above the group;

6. Communicate in vague generalities and confusing terms when defending themselves; and

7. Major on minor issues to the neglect of the truly important ones. (p. 134-135)

As leaders, we need to come under healthy submission (Ephesians 5: 21) and let God have his way in our lives and those we influence. If we insist on having our own way we will become more and more rigid and will not yield to the potter's hand in forming us (Jeremiah 18). Consequently, we will have our own way and miss out on the "better" way (see Hebrews) that leads to transformation and kingdom effectiveness.

6. Pragmatic approach to life and ministry (the end justifies the means).

As we loose touch with the reality that the Kingdom of God is primarily about the means ("being") to the end ("doing"), not the end itself; we will become vulnerable to a pragmatic approach to life and decision-making. The end justifies the means is a common approach, but it is not the kingdom approach.

Again, this happens gradually. We do not decide overnight that we are the moral authority of the universe and that it is O.K. to cut corners or go against God's standards for a greater end. No, we do it gradually through small compromises that pave the way for larger ones. Little by little, we move from integrity to pragmatism, just like the sheep "nibbled itself lost."

When we are under great pressure, it becomes easy for us to cut corners or take the route of least resistance. If we are to maintain our integrity, we must cultivate a life of integrity that is based in submission to the Holy Spirit, obedience to the Word of God, and healthy accountability to others. To not do so will probably lead us where we never intended to go, cost us more than we ever intended on paying, and delay our progress in the things of God (J. Oswald Sanders).

7. Blaming circumstances and others for problems (root of bitterness).

As we begin to reap the bitter results of our increasing pragmatism, we will either have to repent or find dysfunctional ways of coping. We can feel sorry for ourselves, which may lead toward depression, or we can blame circumstances and others. If there is a problem, it cannot have anything to do with us, so it must be circumstantial or personal. We can tend to spiritualize our situation by claiming that we are under a spiritual attack or are being persecuted by unspiritual people.

This response pattern tends, in driven leaders, to result in the type of anger that leads to bitterness (Hebrews 12: 14-15). A learning posture is one of the characteristics of those who finished well. A good rule of thumb for me when things are not going as expected or desired is to ask God if there is anything in me that needs to be dealt with (before blaming circumstances or others as the source of my problems).

My primary upward mentor (Bobby Clinton) once told me that in life and ministry, "You cannot always control your circumstances, but you can always control your attitudes." Ouch, but true! The cartoon figure *Pogo* once said, "I have faced the enemy and he is me!" The blame game does not usually produce anything of value. We may feel better for a few minutes, but we are still faced with our stuff.

Blaming circumstances or others is usually a cop out for not dealing with ourselves. Our failure to learn from adversity stagnates our growth and effectiveness and may necessitate another trip around the mountain (this time with a heavier pack). We need to cultivate a learning posture if we are to live and lead well.

8. Tendency to use people up rather than build them up (viewing people as means rather than the end of ministry).

As we become more pragmatic in our life and leadership decisions, we can also begin to see people as means rather than ends. It has been said, "That before the fall man used things and loved people; while after the fall man loved things and used people." And this tendency can creep into our way of living and leading if we are not careful.

Spiritual gifts, specifically the "equipping gifts" mentioned in Ephesians 4: 11, are to be exercised in love. But if we allow the I Timothy 1: 5 Principle to be compromised in our lives we will not be characterized by love in our relationships.

We will be prone to use people as means to our ends. Over time, people will be hurt, hindered, and even destroyed through our leadership. Rather than "equipping" the saints for ministry we may use them up. When they no longer can perform to our standards we may write them off or get rid of them.

The healthy servant leader views people as the end of ministry. We are to care for, equip, and sponsor others to do even greater works than we can do. Healthy leadership is about empowering others so they can be all that God wants them to be and do. But if we are not careful, allowing ourselves to function in a pragmatic and performance orientation, we may begin to use people up rather than build them up.

9. Neglect of primary relationships (spouse, children, key leaders/staff).

I have already commented on this in the previous chapter. This is another overlapping warning sign that is common to all three of the primary foundational vulnerabilities (burnout, blowout, and plateauing) that we are discussing in this section of the book.

By way of review, remember that the responsibilities and burdens of life and leadership can take a toll on our families, others, and us. We can find ourselves so depleted from stress and over work that we have little emotional energy left for our spouse and children. It is here that we are especially vulnerable to pragmatic thinking and behavior.

We can begin to manipulate our spouse, children, and significant others. In order to maintain our sense of control we may begin to cut corners, tell partial truths, or blame others. If we get a lot of affirmation in leadership and if relationships at home or in the office are difficult, we may give more of our time and energy to non-primary relationships.

We need to have enough left in our emotional tanks for our spouses, children, and significant others. When we drag home dead tired again and again and do not have anything left for the most important people in our lives there is something wrong. If we begin to isolate ourselves from difficult or demanding staff we may loose relational connection with them and loose our ability to influence them in empowering ways.

We may tend to become impatient with others and blame or judge them for our frustrations. We may become manipulative or loose our temper. Either way, we will pay a price in the long haul for our lack of love. Patterns of aggression or passive aggression may be indications that we are relying on our flesh that ultimately leads to frustration, lack of fulfillment, ineffectiveness, and possible blowout.

10. Dependence on personal power rather than spiritual authority (fleshly versus spiritual power).

I tell my students when teaching on leadership, "What is birthed in the flesh must be maintained by the power of the flesh." God does not seen to empower our ideas, even our good ones. My understanding of how the kingdom works is that those things birthed by the Holy Spirit are empowered by the Spirit. God's will is often something that is beyond our resources. It usually takes faith in a supernatural God who is able to keep his promises!

When we are depleted in integrity (or intimacy or faith), we tend to "lean on our own understanding" rather than relying on God (Proverbs 3: 5-6). Over time, we may become so compromised and confused that we start calling our will God's will. When we do this we have to make it happen in our own strength. Trusting God for his will can be demanding enough, but trying to do our version of God's will in our own strength will sooner or later lead to blowout (burnout or plateauing).

Before turning to our Biblical example of blowout, take a break and prayerfully do the self-evaluation found in Appendix C: Blowout Inventory. Again, you may want the input of your spouse, a trusted mentor, or a close friend to help you to honestly assess yourself.

Now, let's look at Samson, a tragic example of someone with incredible gifts and potential who failed to establish and maintain integrity in his life. His story has been played out in the life of far too many over the years. As we look at Samson's life, let us see what we can learn so that we do not end up like him!

Samson: Immorality and Blowout (Judges 13-16)

Text: "Then the Philistines seized him, gouging out his eyes and took him down to Gaza. Binding him with bronze shackles, they set him to grinding in the prison." (Judges 16:21, NIV)

Background:

- Samson means "distinguished, strong"
- He was a Danite and the son of Manoah which means "rest" (13:2)
- Samson led Israel for 20 years (15:20)
- His mother was sterile (13:2) and his birth was miraculous (13:3-5)

- He was called to be a Nazarite (Numbers 6:1-6) from birth (13:5)

    - abstain from grapes, grape juice, alcohol
    - never cut hair on head
    - must not go near or touch dead body

Lack of Integrity, Immorality, and Blowout:

- Samson married a Philistine wife (14:1-2, 10)

- He killed a lion (14:5-6) and ate honey from a carcass (14:8-9)

- He challenged friends with a riddle (14:12-18) and killed 30 men to cover his bet - *"Spirit came upon him in power"*(14:19)

- Samson's wife was given to a friend (14:20)

- Samson takes revenge on the Philistines by tying 300 foxes tails together and lighting them resulting in burning up their fields (15:3-5)

- Philistines took revenge by killing Samson's wife and father-in-law (15:6)

- Samson took revenge on Philistines by killing 1,000 with a donkey's jawbone - *"Spirit came upon him in power"* (15:15)

- Samson spent a night with prostitute in Gaza (16:1) and escaped by carrying the city gates to a hill (16:3)

- Samson fell in love with Delilah (16:4)

- Samson gave Delilah his secret of strength (16:17)

- Samson was captured by Philistines (16:21)

    - seized Samson
    - gouged out his eyes
    - bound him to a grinding wheel in prison

- Samson's hair grew back (16:22) and he got his final revenge by collapsing pillars in a Philistine temple killing himself and many Philistines (16:28-30)

Lessons from the Life of Samson:

- Sin produces death (see James 1:13-15)

- Sin grows if it is not dealt with (see Matthew 5:27-30, II Corinthian 10:3-5)

- God uses sinful people for awhile - "Spirit came upon him in power" (notice that this phrase is no longer included in his exploits after Judges 15:15)

- Samson did not finish well because he did not guard his integrity (see Galatians 6:7-9)

- Disciples must take their vows seriously – Samson violated the conditions of his Nazarite vow (see Numbers 6:1-6)

- Character is essential for long haul effectiveness in life and ministry (see John 15:1-8)

In this chapter we have taken a look at blowout and the integrity cracks that can lead us to a life of moral failure like Samson's. We have described the importance of cultivating integrity, how integrity cracks develop, and ten warning signs of blowout. In the next chapter we will take a look at what happens when we fail to learn to live from faith to faith (Romans 1: 17) and describe the 10 warning signs of plateauing.

Evaluation and Application

1. What is the definition of blowout? Why is establishing, maintaining, and enlarging our foundation of integrity important for navigating the challenges of mid-life if we want to finish well? How would you rate your integrity? What areas do you need to improve and how are you going to go about it?

2. What integrity cracks did you discover in your foundation? If you have any, how are you going to repair them?

3. How did you do on the Blowout Inventory? What are the specific area(s) that you are vulnerable? How are you going to strengthen these areas and guard yourself from becoming more vulnerable to blowout?

4. What did you learn from studying the life of Samson? What lessons do you need to apply to your own life and how do you plan to do so?

Chapter 6

10 Warning Signs of Plateauing

I (Paul) have seen so many good leaders loose their nerve and play it safe as they enter mid-life. They once were innovators and risk takers, but over time they became more careful, even resistant to taking risks. They once were idealistic and now they are the status quo. This is called plateauing. I will share two stories here because plateauing can occur in the context of failure or success. The following stories are compilations of several real life situations that will illustrate how we can become complacent and settle for less than God's best.

Sid and Sally – Hurt and Failure

First, let's take a look at the story of Sid (not his real name). Sid graduated from Bible college (or seminary) in his twenties. He had sensed a calling to vocational ministry in his teens at a summer youth camp and had pursued his dream since then. He met Sally (not her real name) while in school and they were married during the summer after graduation and right before Sid's first full-time ministry assignment as a youth pastor at a small, but growing, church in a suburban community in another state.

Sid and Sally were excited about their new life together and the opportunity to serve in this new ministry situation. Both Sid and Sally had taken out school loans to pay for their education and were a little concerned about how they were going to make it financially, but they were optimistic that everything would work out. After all, they were in love and were following God's call.

Soon after Sid and Sally relocated to their new church home, the pressures of relocation, starting a new marriage, and the seemingly unending demands of ministry began to press in. Sally had found a part-time job at a local day care center and Sid was very busy trying to get the youth group off the ground. Sally was lonely and Sid was busy. They tried to make sure that they made time for regular date nights, but often that involved going together to an event involving kids from the youth group with coffee afterwards.

There was so much to do and Sid's days got longer and longer and his time off got less and less. The senior pastor at the church was a go-getter and had great hopes that a successful youth group would attract more families and grow the church. Sid's inexperience began to show and the senior pastor began to become impatient and at time micro managed Sid. Sid began to struggle with his confidence and sense of calling. Sally was feeling lonely, frustrated, and was beginning to resent the expectations and demands that the church was placing on them.

She felt as though there was an expectation that she be a full time volunteer at the church – youth ministry, women's ministry, volunteering in the nursery. And not only this, but student loans had now kicked in and they were having a hard time making it financially.

By now, Sid was feeling pressure from the senior pastor because the youth group was not growing as fast as expected and his wife because he was spending more and more time away from home to be involved in youth events. Sally began to say no to some expectations at the church and distance herself emotionally. The senior pastor perceived this as a lack of commitment and another indication that Sid may not be the leader he had hoped for.

After a year of growing frustration, hurt, and failure to measure up to expectations, Sid and Sally resigned from the church and moved to another community were Sid took a sales job and they got on with their lives. They saved their marriage, faithfully attended a local church, raised their family, got out of debt after several years, had some success in their jobs, and were planning for retirement with the hope that they might be able to serve as volunteers at a local church camp during summers.

Not a bad life. It could have been a lot worse! They did the best they could with the hand they were dealt, but there was always lingering doubts for Sid, "Was this God's best?" "Did I turn my back on God's call to vocational Christian service?" "Why have I lost my passion for service and life?" "Why am I so preoccupied with retirement?" "Why has life turned out to be such a disappointment (even though I have a lot of things to be thankful for)?"

Bubba and Betty – Success

Next, let's take a look at Bubba (not his real name). Bubba was a classmate of Sid's at Bible college (or seminary). They were friends, but not close. Sid was a very good student and Bubba was only an average student, but Bubba was exceptionally good with people. It seemed as though Bubba was a people magnet – wherever he went he could attract a group.

He was outgoing, fun to be around, and always doing crazy things. Bubba was not a very deep thinker. He was more of a go-with-the-flow; make it up as you go type of guy.

He too took a youth pastor position after graduation. As a single youth pastor in a similar type of church as the one Sid was serving in, he was an immediate success. He worked tirelessly, especially on developing relationships, and grew the youth group to over 100 within his first year. He struggled some with planning, budget, and follow through but the senior pastor at the church coached him and provided resources as he could.

After the first year, Bubba married his college (seminary) sweetheart Betty (not her real name) and they started their new life together. There were adjustments and challenges during their first year of marriage, but with the continued growth of the youth group, everything seemed to be going well. After three years at the church, the youth group was over 150 and Bubba was being asked to share at regional youth leader's events about his success and even being contacted about new ministry opportunities.

After five years of continuing success and expanding responsibilities (he was now an Assistant Pastor) at the church, Bubba and Betty decide to start a new church in a neighboring community. This too grew and after another five years, there were about 500 adults, plus kids and youth, who regularly attended Sunday services.

This led to a building project and all the demands of fund raising, working with contractors, board members, and expectant members. The building project took longer and cost more than expected, but Bubba was able to see the project through to completion (and the church continued to grow).

By this time, Bubba had gained the attention and favor of leaders in his association of churches and was being asked to speak and serve on boards. He enjoyed the attention and the opportunities to take a "legitimate" break from the pressures associated with his growing local church.

Bubba was in his late 40s, he was a successful senior pastor, traveling and speaking on the conference circuit, writing a book, and serving on national boards. He also had led the church in another building project, but this time had not seen the continued growth that he saw with the first one. In fact, the church seemed to be plateauing and there were growing pressures financially because of the large loans that were taken out for the two building projects.

Not all was going well on the home front and he needed to make important decisions about staff, salaries, budget, etc. Bubba began to second guess himself, travel more, and put off critical decisions (that at one time had been easier for him to make). Bubba felt stuck in his circumstances and could not see a way though. He began to ask, "What is going on?" "Why is this happening to me?" "Why aren't things working like they used to?" "Is my time up here, but I have so many responsibilities and people looking to me for answers?"

Both Sid and Bubba have become plateaued. That does not mean that they are bad people or even poor leaders. They have both become stuck in their circumstances and have flat-lined in their faith. They are plateaued.

What is Plateauing?

Once again, there are probably some pretty technical definitions for plateauing, but I like to think of it in terms of the "inability to continue following God in faithful and fruitful ways because of a lack of trust in God going forward." This definition suggests,

1. Inability – we lack resources necessary to face real life/ministry challenges.

2. Following God – our primary relationship and purpose in life.

3. Faithful – we need to cultivate the ability to hear God's voice and obey.

4. Fruitful – we are meant to reproduce "in kind" and leave a legacy for generations to come and for eternity.

BECAUSE OF:

5. Lack of Trust – lack of confidence in God and selective faithfulness to him resulting in stagnation in our development as leaders and loss of spiritual authority to influence others.

Plateauing can happen within the context of unresolved hurt and a sense of failure or ongoing success. Plateauing is subtler than either burnout or blowout because there might not be the disastrous consequences that are associated with the others. A closer look at the implications of personal plateauing on organizations will reveal how this subtle condition can have a profoundly negative impact.

Personal and Organizational Plateauing

Let me lay some groundwork here about organizational dynamics that can play a major role in our understanding of the process and impact of plateauing. Like people, organizations have a life cycle. Simply put, unless organizations "cheat history" by reinventing themselves before they plateau, they will begin to decline. The typical life cycle of an organization looks something like this:

Diagram 4: Historical Drift Curve

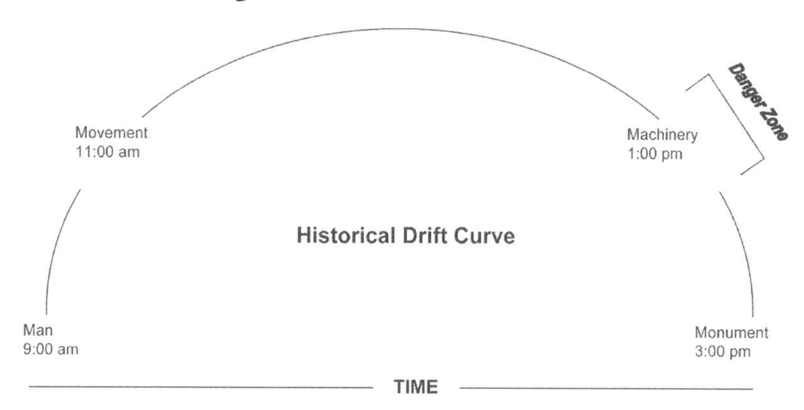

Sociologists who study organization have identified a pattern to how organizations develop over time. The time sequences between these stages change from organization to organization, but the critical issue related to the future health of an organization has to do with whether or not they can change appropriately with changing times. They must "cheat history" or jump the sigmoid curve if they are to stay healthy, relevant, and profitable.

Diagram 5: Jumping the Sigmoid Curve

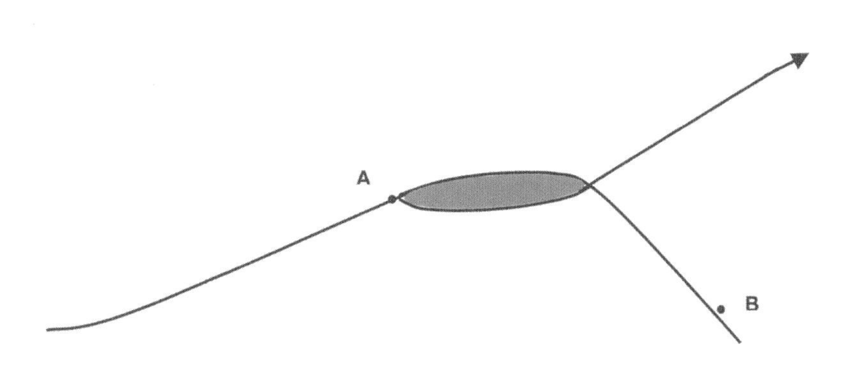

The research by Jim Collins, *How the Mighty Fall*, is very insightful here. In the past, many organizational experts believed that plateauing and decline occurred because of the impact of poor leadership and bureaucracy after the founding entrepreneurial leader transitioned. What Collins discovered is that the DNA for plateauing and decline actually begins much earlier than previously thought. He states (p. 20-21):

"Great enterprises can become insulated by successes; accumulated momentum can carry an enterprise forward, for awhile, even if its leaders make poor decisions or loose discipline. Stage 1 [of five stages of decline] kicks in when people become arrogant, regarding success virtually as an entitlement, and they lose sight of the true underlying factors that created success in the first place."

Wow! Do you see the connection between personal and organizational plateauing? I describe arrogance as "trusting in self" with two primary manifestations in plateauing:

1. Self-preservation
2. Self-promotion

Self-preservation tends to be associated with hurt and failure (the example of Sid), while self-promotion tends to be associated with ongoing success (the example of Bubba). Either way, arrogance or "trusting in self" breaks down the faith dynamic so essential in healthy, maturing Christian discipleship and leadership.

Faith Dynamic

Back in the 1980s I was on a church staff that was led by John Wimber, the founder of Vineyard Christian Fellowship. He would occasionally ask us during staff meetings how we spelled faith. His answer was RISK, because he wanted us to understand that faith as a leader involved more than taking care of business. It also involved the dynamics of vision and risk. I agree with this, but have just a little different take on it. I now spell faith TRUST, because I have learned that faith is primarily relational – that taking risks as a leader involves vision that comes from God who is able to keep his promises, his way!

Let me explain. Faith (*pistis*) according to Vine (*Vine's Complete Expository Dictionary*, p. 222) means:

> "'firm persuasion,' a conviction based upon hearing (akin to peitho, 'to persuade'), is used in the NT always of 'faith in God or Christ, or things spiritual.' The word is used of (a) **trust**... (b) trust-worthiness... (c) the contents of belief...
>
> (d) assurance... (e) a pledge of fidelity... **The main element of 'faith' is its relationship to the invisible God...** "(**bold** added for emphasis)

According to the author of Hebrews, "faith is being sure of what we hope for and certain of what we do not see" (Hebrews 11: 1, NIV). We also know that "without faith it is impossible to please God..." (Hebrews 11: 6a, NIV). Abraham is used in Hebrews 11 as one of the primary examples of faith and faithfulness in the Old Testament. In a parallel passage in Romans we are given an inside view of Abraham's faith:

> "Against all hope [he was old and his wife was barren]... he did not waver through unbelief regarding the promise of God [for a son], but was strengthened in his faith and gave glory to God, being **fully persuaded that God had power to do what he promised.**" Romans 3: 18-21, NIV (**bold** added for emphasis)

Let me show you how this works in the following diagram that I call the "faith/vision cycle":

Diagram 6: Faith/Vision Cycle

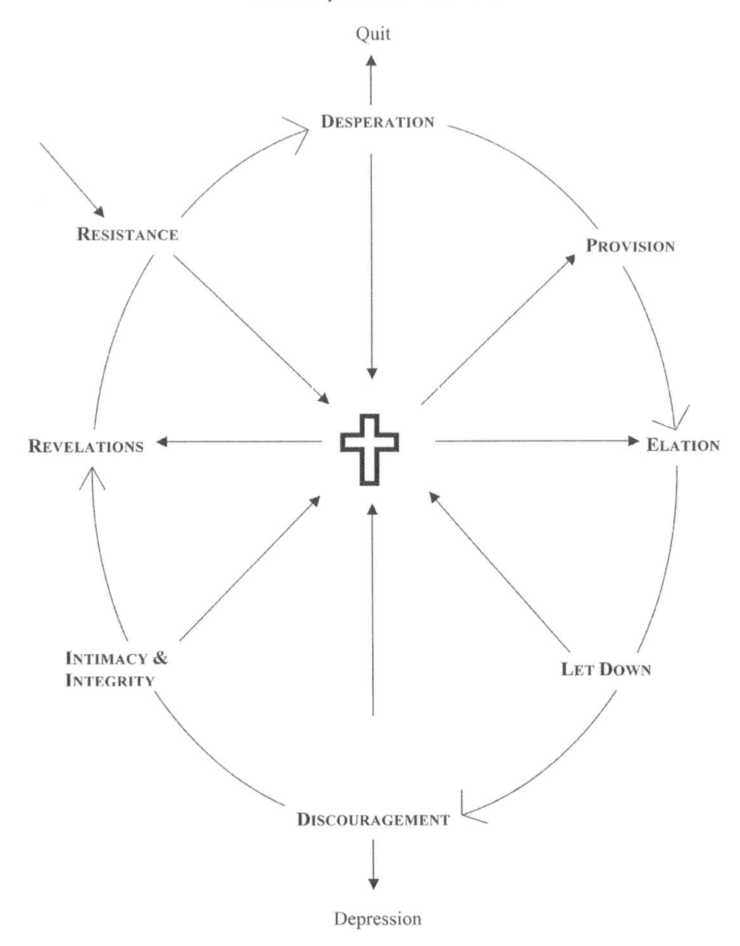

We start with revelation (Bible insights or hearing the voice of God) and begin to step out in faith (obedience). Done deal, right? No, it does not seem to work that way. I have learned that with faith (obedience) will come resistance. Personally, resistance may come from our flesh, the world, or the enemy. As a leader, resistance may come from these as well as from the people you are leading. Either way, in all likelihood, you will experience resistance as you progress in faith.

If we continue in faith (obedience), eventually we will see God's provision. Often times, God's provision comes when we are at the end of our own confidence, resources, or abilities. This is because God wants us to learn to live and lead by faith. He wants us to learn how to experience what I call "supernatural-natural living." Remember Paul's words about weakness and strength (II Corinthians 12: 10)?

Notice here that there are two primary points at which we tend to be most vulnerable to giving up or giving in: desperation and discouragement. Desperation can lead to self-doubt that can lead to quitting – "It is just too hard." We do not have the resources to keep going, so we quit. It is at this point where our paradigm is challenged and we can learn how to rely on God's faithfulness to provide!

The second point of vulnerability occurs after we have experienced God's faithful provision. We are initially energized (elated) by seeing God come through. We were hot wired by God for this kind of faith and it is awesome. "Yes! Praise God, I was made for this!!!!" But we, in our humanity, cannot stay here for very long. There will eventually be a let down and we can become vulnerable to discouragement (see the story of Elijah in I Kings 19 for an example of this). Discouragement can lead to self-pity that can lead to full on depression if we are not careful.

In both cases, the primary issue for us to learn to deal with is the weakness of our humanity (self or flesh) and our need to learn how to rely upon God for intimacy and integrity that can lead to further or future revelation and the cycle starts all over again. That is why Paul talks about faith leading to faith (Romans 1: 17). Today's faithfulness is prerequisite for tomorrow's challenges! Faith (trust) is dynamic and leads to personal transformation and a deeper understanding of who God is and how he works.

All of us are prone to rationalization, projection, and settling for formulas instead of learning how to live from faith to faith. These defense mechanisms are subtle and often acceptable in our culture, even in the Christian sub-culture.

Over time, this defensive posture will betray the reality that we are living and leading in our own strength rather than submitting to God by faith. By default, our defense mechanisms betray the fact that we are trusting in ourselves rather than God. If we do not break this pattern, we will eventually find ourselves stuck in our circumstances and the subtle, but devastating consequences of plateauing will begin to define our lives and leadership and our impact in the organizations that we are apart of.

What are the "trust cracks" that feed the pattern of self-preservation and self-promotion that is at the core of plateauing?

Trust Cracks: Sources of Plateauing

Again, the Bible gives us insight and wisdom concerning the "trust crack" that can develop in our spiritual formation foundation that can lead to plateauing. James describes two type of wisdom: heavenly and earthly wisdom. Let's take a closer look at what James has to say about these two types of wisdom:

> "Who is wise and understanding among you? Let him show it by his good life, by deeds done in the humility that comes from wisdom. But if you harbor bitter envy and selfish ambition in your hearts, do not boast about it or deny the truth. Such 'wisdom' does not come down from heaven but is earthly, unspiritual, of the devil." (James 3: 13-15, NIV)

So, there are two types of wisdom that have different sources, and eventually, different outcomes. Let's look at the source and outcomes of these.

1. Heavenly Wisdom's source is God's truth (verse 14) and its outcome is (verses 17-18):

* pure
* peace-loving
* considerate
* submissive
* full of mercy
* good fruit
* impartial
* sincere

2. Earthly Wisdom's source is the devil (verse 15) and its outcome is (verses14-16):

* bitter envy
* selfish ambition
* boastful
* unspiritual
* disorder
* evil practice

This is quite a contrast. Now, it may take a long time for the differences in these two types of wisdom to manifest, but eventually they will (see Galatians 6: 7-8). Over the years, I have learned from my own experience and that of others that there are major trust cracks that we need to be aware of and counteract by God's grace if we are to avoid plateauing and manifest the heavenly wisdom that James talked about. These include:

1. **Failure** – Everyone experiences failure from time to time, but repeated failure, humiliating failure, or the hurts associated with failure can build up and caused doubts, diminished self-confidence, and ultimately a lack of trust in God. It is easy for most of us to focus on the negative feelings, perceptions, and consequences associated with failure. We feel like we did something wrong, are inadequate

in some way, or have let others down. All of this can be a pretty heavy load to bear. But there is more to failure than this for those who have faith. John Maxwell calls it "failing forward." I like this concept because it reminds us that God can do something in and through us regardless of our weakness, inadequacies, or even laziness. We can learn from our mistakes and grow in grace and effectiveness.

2. **Rejection** - This can be a real time bomb for leaders because it attacks the very core of who we are. Most of us struggle with some sort of insecurity. We have a vague sense that we are inadequate or even worthless (or at least not as valuable in God's eyes as other more talented or successful leaders). This may manifest itself in lack of initiative or trying too hard which can put other people off. We get rejected, which reinforces our self-concept, and we can begin to live with the expectation that sooner or later we will be rejected because of our deficiencies as a person.

This is more than a performance issue – it relates to the value of our self. Again, God's intention is to value us through his love and grace so that we can experience his love and love others. This is difficult for many of us to experience because we have been rejected by significant others. This can be especially difficult if rejection has come from Christian people. "How can we trust God if we cannot trust his people?" Fortunately, God is not like some of his people. He loves us no matter what and there is self-worth and fulfillment in living in his acceptance!

3. **Deep Processing** - I will spend a little more time on this because it has many ramifications related to trust cracks. J. Robert Clinton, in his *Clinton's Biblical Leadership Commentary*, defines deep processing as "process items that intensively work on deepening the maturity of a leader" (p. 684). Process items involve life circumstances and relationships that result in character development, skill development, and expanded potential. They are providential in nature, designed by God to help develop a leader's capacity.

Deep processing is a special category of Clinton's list of process items, but they may overlap with each other in the complexities of life and leadership experiences and relationships. For our purposes here, I have adapted Clinton's findings and come up with the following list of deep processing items:

1. Life transitions
2. Life and leadership crises
3. Life and leadership conflict
4. Leadership backlash
5. Isolation
6. Spiritual warfare
7. Brokenness

Let's briefly define and describe each of these. Several of the following definitions are taken from the Glossary in Clinton's *The Making of a Leader*.

1. *Life transitions* – Change happens to all of us sooner or later. Life transitions occur during times of major changes such as death of a loved one, becoming "empty nesters", loss of a job, retirement, etc. Along with these situational life transitions there are developmental life transitions that we must navigate as we age and become more mature. Example: Paul

2. *Life and leadership crises* – "Process items that refer to special intense situations in life, which are used by God to test and teach dependence on Him" (p. 238). "A specialized form of a Crisis process item, referring to a time of crisis characterized by intense pressure in which the meaning and purpose of life are searched out, and the leader has experienced God in a new way as the Source of life, the Sustainer of life, and the Focus of life" (p. 246). Example: Peter

3. *Life and leadership conflict* – "Instances in a leader's life in which God uses conflict, whether personal or ministry related, to develop the leader in dependence upon God, faith, and insights relating to personal life and ministry" (p. 237). "A process item referring to those instances in ministry in which a leader learns either positive or negative lessons about the nature of conflict, possible ways to resolve conflict, possible ways to avoid conflict, ways to creatively use conflict, and how to see conflict in terms of God's processing of the leader's inner life" (p. 249). Example: Paul and Barnabas

4. *Leadership backlash* – "A process item describing the condition when followers react against a course of action taken by a leader; usually due to unforeseen complications arising after the followers have previously approved of the action" (p. 245). Example: Moses (Exodus 14)

5. *Isolation* – "A maturity factor item in which a leader is separated from normal ministry, while in the natural context in which the ministry has been occurring, usually for an extended time, and thus experiences God in a new and deeper way" (p. 244-245). Example: Elijah (I Kings 19)

6. *Spiritual warfare* – There is a real devil and he is an adversary of God and his purposes. Leaders may face times when they encounter spiritual realities that may hinder their life and leadership progress. We are told several times in the Bible that we do not live in a natural world, but a natural/supernatural world where we need to learn how to do spiritual warfare (Ephesians 6: 10-20). Example: Daniel

7. *Brokenness* – A process by which God brings us to the end of ourselves in order for us to learn to live and lead under

the control of his spirit. There may be several breakings before brokenness is accomplished. The primary fruit of brokenness is love (I Timothy 1: 5), which is manifest in humility (I Peter 5: 6). Example: Joseph

Deep processing can take us to levels of understanding, maturity, and spiritual authority that cannot happen any other way. God initiates deep processing because he wants to take us deeper into himself and his resources for our fulfillment and effectiveness. If we endure during deep processing, we will experience some of the following:

1. A deeper sense of God's love.

2. A greater appropriation of the fruit of the spirit.

3. A greater appreciation of God's faithfulness.

4. A new way of looking at life and leadership (paradigm change).

5. A greater understanding of God's majesty and holiness.

6. A greater level of intimacy and integrity.

7. A greater capacity to function in spiritual authority.

8. A greater freedom from sin and fleshly patterns.

9. A greater realization of the fear of God.

10. A greater sensitivity to the "voice of God."

11. A greater appreciation of others.

12. A greater passion for God and his purposes.

13. A greater sense of giftedness and calling.

14. A more focused life.

15. A greater capacity to finish well in life and leadership.

These and many other outcomes are possible if we can learn to submit to God in the midst of deep processing. Remember Job and how God transformed him and blessed him with a double portion of what he had lost during his "severe mercy." For more information about deep processing see the Resource section (*Deep Processing: Maturing Through Really Hard Times*).

4. **Success** – Too much success and premature promotion can be deadly for faith. We can begin to take ourselves more seriously than we should and gradually think that we have it all figured out or are somehow critical to God's purposes. This is dangerous ground to be on! Sooner or later, our foundation will be exposed. If we have built success on formula or the force of our personality and gifts, we will be exposed for our shallowness and lack of mature substance. Learning how to be faithful in difficult times (deep processing) can be good for us and save us from the frustration and failure of self-promotion.

5. **Materialism** - Living by sight, rather than by faith, can lead to materialism – a dependence on position, power, popularity, or possessions for a sense of well being. If our acceptance and security is not based in our relationship with God we will tend to play it safe or act in our own interests. Over time, we can find ourselves buying into and maintaining a status quo that is compromised at best and spiritually deadly at the worst. It is good to have to trust God for provision, productivity, and his promises. As we do, we grow in our trust and confidence that he is able to keep his promises!

10 Warning Signs of Plateauing

The following list of warning signs is based on my experience and observations from working with leaders over the years. It is not inspired or all encompassing. It is practical and meant to serve as a means to help us evaluate ourselves so that we can take corrective measures before we plateau. Prayerfully consider the following warning signs and let the Holy Spirit "lead you into all truth" in this matter. Warning signs for potential plateauing may include:

1. A series of failures leading to a lack of confidence (in God) and self-preservation; or a series of successes leading to self-confidence and self-promotion.

We all face ups and downs in life – failures and successes. How we process them is what is important here. Attitude is everything. There are potential lessons to be learned in failure and success. Each provides unique opportunities for growth and maturing.

If we do not establish, maintain, and enlarge our spiritual formation foundation on trusting faith, we become vulnerable to self-preservation or self-promotion. This occurs subtly and over time, but can lead to plateauing and missing opportunities to trust God for greater life transformation and leadership impact.

Living in humility is key here. Whether we experience failure or success, it is not ultimately about us. As much as our experiences might hurt or feel good, we need to remember that God loves us and is working in the midst of our circumstances to help us grow in faith so that we can eventually experience fulfillment and greater fruitfulness.

2. Confusion and frustration about God's will and an eventual loss of assurance in God's calling and purpose in life and ministry.

As we encounter ups and down and subtly begin to become more self-focused, we will experience confusion and frustration about God's will. At times, there is a very subtle difference between a "good" idea and a God idea. One letter makes a huge difference over the long haul.

I am told that a sailor or pilot have to check their instruments regularly as they sail or fly long distances. Just being off course a degree can lead to the wrong destination over time. So it is with our lives and leadership. Unfortunately, many leaders get caught up in the momentum of their own pattern of failure or success and do not stop long enough to get God's perspective. Humbly practicing spiritual disciplines and having periodic times of prayerful self-evaluation can help keep us on course. This helps break patterns of self-preservation or self-promotion.

3. Loss of idealism and passion for something better and a default to maintenance and keeping the peace.

Many of us started out in ministry or leadership wanting to have an impact or change something that was wrong or ineffective. Young leaders usually are idealistic, naive, and inexperienced in leadership and change dynamics. This is not necessarily bad or wrong – it is probably more an issue of maturity than anything else.

We share our ideas or try to initiate change and experience negativity or resistance and we get frustrated or beat down. Again, this is an opportunity to learn about leadership, how effective change happens, and ourselves. Unfortunately, for many, we give up our idealism over time because we get discouraged or warn down. Over time, we can default to a maintenance mode where keeping the peace is more expedient than persevering through these challenges to see God's will accomplished.

This is where knowing that we are pursuing God's will, not just our good ideas, is so critical. I have learned that the implementation of good ideas depends on me, while the implementation of God's will depends on his provision in his time. Doing God's will involves faith that fuels true passion.

4. Looking to something outside of your current situation for fulfillment (i.e. another relationship, another position, a promotion, etc.).

Remember the faith dynamic diagram that I shared earlier in this chapter? It is between the revelation (God's will) and provision stages that we will most likely experience resistance and desperation. This is necessary and good because it gives us an opportunity to trust God. God's will always involves trusting him for provision! It is during this time of resistance and desperation that leaders are vulnerable to trust cracks that can lead to plateauing. It is too difficult; we cannot keep going in our own strength.

We look for distractions or ways to prop ourselves up and miss an opportunity to die anew to our self-centeredness. The flesh does not die easily. It will act religiously or throw a tantrum, but it will not die unless we submit to God in this process. I have learned that if you are not broken, you are not much good for the king and the advancement of his kingdom.

5. A growing appetite for materialism and creature comforts as a basis of worth and security (whether you have money or not).

Our flesh or self-centeredness needs to be fed if it is to remain in control of our lives. One of the most potent ways that we feed the flesh is through materialism. By materialism, I do not mean having or wanting more stuff, although that is part of it. Materialism is a value system that claims worth and fulfillment in the pursuit or accumulation of stuff. It is the prominent worldview in Western cultures and has infiltrated the Christian sub-culture is subtle and superficial ways.

As trust cracks begin to enlarge in our spiritual formation foundation, we become more vulnerable to this counterfeit worldview, which can rob us of abundant life and ongoing opportunities to trust God and be generous toward others (especially the needy). What is especially dangerous about materialism is that it is fear based and never truly satisfies. It promises much and delivers very little, leading us to a sort of addiction to the newest, best, coolest, hottest, etc. Materialism can make us shallow and superficial over time.

6. A growing unwillingness to make the hard decisions (laissez-faire approach) or making the hard decisions without due process (authoritarian approach).

If we buy into the subtle or superficial expressions of materialism, we may gradually find ourselves needing to maintain the status quo. Rocking the boat may now cost us personally. It might mean that our position of influence or current life-style might have to change. At this point we have to sure up the system that feeds us.

Depending on our personalities and life experience, we may tend to let things go or become controlling in our decision-making. Either way, we can become advocates for the way it is and miss an opportunity to trust God to make changes that will lead to a better day for those we are suppose to be serving. Over time, we can become the gatekeepers for the status quo because change would cost us too much.

7. Covering your backside, taking care of your own needs first and foremost, and becoming more and more cynical.

Over time, we can become so self absorbed that we develop patterns of self-preservation or self-promotion that can lead to covering our backside and becoming cynical. We may find ourselves having lost our passion and defending our turf. This is hard and draining work that may lead to us projecting our own compromised situation on others.

We may begin to get a little paranoid, wondering who is out to get us or who wants our position. This is pretty cynical stuff. Rather than seeing potential in younger emerging leaders we may see them as a threat or as ambitious. Either way, we may miss some life empowering opportunities to help them develop. We may become like the folks who resisted us and frustrated us when we were young and idealistic.

8. Becoming more critical or passive-aggressive of other's creative, change oriented ideas, especially if they mean change, loss of control or influence, or more work for you.

If we are not careful, we may find ourselves throwing spears at the next generation of Davids (I Samuel 18-19). Our spears can manifest themselves as open criticism or passive-aggressive politics in the boardroom. We can become like the folks who resisted and rejected us when we were younger. Rather than empowering others and the organizations that we are suppose to be serving, we can become impediments to the development of others and organizational change that may be necessary for future health and effectiveness.

9. Holding on to current positions, even if you are unfulfilled and unfruitful, because you do not know what to do next or are afraid of the uncertainty of stepping out in faith.

Knowing when to pass the baton on to another leader is always challenging, but for those who are plateaued, it is especially difficult. They may dump and run or hang on much longer than they should. Either option will result in unnecessary confusion, hurt, and conflict.

Healthy, mature leaders have a transition plan that helps maximize the potential for those they serve and the organizations that they lead. They practice passing the baton over the years leading up to their ultimate transition. They have a legacy of empowering other leaders whether they stay in the organization or eventually serve someplace else.

Hanging on too long or poor transitions are symptomatic of plateaued leaders because their focus has been on themselves and their future rather than on God and his preferred future for the people involved. Poor transitions reveal our hearts and lead to negative legacies.

10. Growing tendency to isolate from people of faith and hang with the veterans of the organization that are hanging on until retirement.

Over time, we may begin to isolate ourselves from those who are demonstrating faith in their lives and leadership. We may find ourselves saying, "Just give them a few years and they will come down to earth!" Wow, how sad. May it never be! But unfortunately, it happens way too much. We may find ourselves later in life surrounded by the type of leaders who resisted us or rejected us when we were younger. Do you see how sad and tragic this is?

There is a life-giving dynamic in the faith of younger leaders that can remind us and refresh us, as we grow older. As we approach convergence and afterglow, we will have opportunities to encourage and empower others through faith and in the process remain faithful and finish well.

Before turning to our Biblical example of plateauing, take a break and prayerfully do the self-evaluation found in Appendix D: Plateauing Inventory. Again, you may want to gain the perspective of others as you honestly evaluate how you are doing in trusting God and avoiding plateauing.

Now, let's look at Gideon, a tragic example of someone who seemed to start well but never established mature faithfulness in his life and leadership. His story has been played out in the lives of far too many over the years. As we look at Gideon's life, let us see what we can learn about faith and plateauing so that we do not end up like him!

Gideon: Failure to Move From Fleece to Faith

Text: "Gideon made the gold into an ephod, which he placed in Ophrah, his town. All Israel prostituted themselves by worshipping it there, and it became a snare to Gideon and his family." (Judges 8: 27)

Context: Gideon was a Judge in Israel after seven years of oppression at the hands of the Midianites (Judges 6: 1-6) because Israel "cried to the Lord because of Midian" (6:7). He defeated the Midianites and there was peace in Israel for forty years (8: 28). After he died, the Israelites quickly returned to Baal worship (8: 33).

Overview of Gideon's Life and Leadership:

* Gideon ("feller, hewer, smiter") was the least in the weakest clan of the tribe of Manasseh (Judges 6: 15)
* He was visited by an angel while threshing wheat in a winepress to keep it from the Midianites (6: 11)
* The angel called Gideon a "mighty warrior" because God was with him (6: 12)
* The Lord commissioned Gideon - "Save Israel out of Midian's hand" (6: 14)
* Gideon asked for a sign (6: 17) and God miraculously provided fire as confirmation (6: 21)
* Gideon built an alter, cut down an Asherah pole for fire wood, and sacrificed a bull (6: 25-27)
* The men of Gideon's town confronted him about this, but his father defended him (6: 28-32)

* While the Midianites, Amalekites, and others joined together to attack Israel (6: 33), the Spirit of the Lord came upon Gideon and he called the Israelites together to defend themselves (6: 34-35)
* While waiting for them to arrive, Gideon asked God for a "fleece" twice as confirmation that God was with him (6: 36-4)
* The Lord had Gideon reduce the size of his army until there were only 300 left (7: 6-7) and armed them with torches, jars, and trumpets (7: 16)
* The Lord woke Gideon up one night and had him go down to the edge of the Midianite camp where he overheard a man telling another about a dream that Gideon would defeat them (7: 13-14)
* Gideon and his 300 men defeated the Midianites (7: 21-8: 21)
* The Israelites asked Gideon to rule them (8: 22) but he refused (8: 23)
* Instead, Gideon asked for gold earrings from the plunder (8: 24)
* They gave Gideon over seventeen hundred shekels (8: 26) of jewelry from which he made a gold ephod (8: 27) that the Israelites worshipped (8: 27)
* The ephod became as snare for Gideon and his family (8: 27)
* After Gideon died, the Israelites quickly returned to Baal worship (8: 33) and did not show kindness to Gideon's family (8: 35)

Lessons From the Life of Gideon:

1. Gideon viewed himself as insignificant, but was open to God's purpose as a deliverer.

2. Gideon had immature faith and needed a lot of confirmation (sign, two fleeces, and a dream) to obey God.

3. Ultimately, Gideon obeyed God and saw a great victory over the Midianites.

4. Gideon probably showed false humility by refusing the offer to rule Israel, but asking instead for gold. Gold was a source of wealth and power.

5. Gideon's insecurity probably caused him to build the Ephod (symbol of God's anointing) that the Israelites worshipped.

6. Gideon never moved from the fleece (immature faith) to trust (mature faith) in God's ongoing provision.

7. After his death the Israelites returned to idolatry and mistreated his family. He did not leave a lasting legacy.

In this chapter we have taken a look at plateauing and the trust cracks that can lead us to a life of stagnation like Gideon's. We have described the importance of cultivating faith (TRUST), how trust cracks develop, and ten warning signs of plateauing. In the next chapter we will take a look at how I have used my understanding of the I Timothy 1: 5 Principle to pro-actively establish, maintain, and enlarge my spiritual formation foundation (purity of heart, clarity of conscience, sincerity of faith) to become a more loving person and effective leader.

Evaluation and Application

1. What is the definition of plateauing? Why is establishing, maintaining, and enlarging our foundation of faith (TRUST) important for navigating the challenges of midlife if we want to finish well? How would you rate your faithfulness? What areas do you need to improve and how are you going to go about it?

2. What did you learn about personal and organizational plateauing? What did you learn about faith dynamics? What insights have you gained that will help you remain faithful in your personal life and organizational leadership?

3. What trust cracks did you discover in your foundation? If you have any, how are you going to repair them?

4. How did you do on the Plateauing Inventory? What are the specific area(s) that you are vulnerable? How are you going to strengthen these areas and guard yourself from becoming more vulnerable to plateauing?

5. What did you learn from studying the life of Gideon? What lessons do you need to apply to your own life and how do you plan to do so?

Chapter 7

Establishing Disciplines of Faithfulness

I (Paul) was in my early 40's. I had made some major life and career decisions over the previous few years that had changed the course of my life. I had left a career in higher education for full-time Christian service and found myself at the end of my rope.

During the past few years I had been forced out or asked to leave three ministries and I was currently out of work. I found myself in a situation where I had lost confidence in my abilities and was not even able to provide financially for my family. It was a time of utter despair and desperation.

My motivation in all of this was a desire to follow God more fully. I was trying to let God do a work of transformation, I was trying to learn to be more dependent on God; but it was not working out (at least, the way I had thought it would). As my wife and I sought God in our desperation, we felt a sense of his presence and peace but our circumstances seemed to keep getting worse.

The Phone Call

And then, the phone rang. I answered and the person on the other end introduced himself as Jeff Farmer, President of Eugene Bible College in Oregon. He said that they had a teaching position open and were looking for someone with a graduate degree in counseling (preferably a doctorate) and Youth With A Mission (YWAM) Discipleship Training School (DTS) experience to teach at the college and develop a discipleship training program for freshman.

There were probably a handful of folks who met these criteria and I was one of them. I had never met the man and only knew vaguely about the college. He had been pretty creative and persistent in his process of hunting down candidates and had located me after several dead ends.

He asked me whether I would be interested in interviewing for the position. I tried not to be too eager and told him that my wife and I would pray about it and get back to him. To cut to the chase, we let him know that we were interested and within a few days found ourselves in Eugene, OR interviewing for the position.

During the interview process I was pretty honest about the last couple of years. Although I had a great looking resume with outstanding references, I also knew that I had some baggage. I told Jeff that along with my references that he probably needed to talk with a couple of people who might not be so high on me.

The interview lasted for a couple of days, which gave Jeff time to call my references and the couple of other folks who I had encouraged him to talk to. At our final meeting, Jeff started the conversation with, "I have talked to all of the people you suggested I talk to and have had some pretty interesting conversations!" I thought to myself, "I bet you have and knowing what you now know my candidacy is history!"

Jeff next said, "You are either a gifted and talented person who has some tragic flaws that cause you to self destruct" or "You are a gifted and talented person who has not yet found the right place to serve." My bet would have been on the first assessment, but he went on to say, "I have prayed about you and sense that it is the later, will you take this position at EBC and join my team?" I could not believe it! It was as though God was saying, "I have not given up on you (in spite of all of the drama these past couple of years)!"

Little did I know at the time that I would end up as part of Jeff's team as he transitioned from the college to the Presidency of the association of churches that sponsored the college. I ended up servicing with Jeff for twenty years until his retirement in 2011. We served well together and developed a wonderful friendship during those challenging and rewarding years. What I learned from this experience is that if I will attend to the disciplines of faithfulness, God's intervention is just a phone call away!

Five Disciplines of Faithfulness for Navigating Mid-Life Ministry

I like Eugene Peterson phrase "a long obedience in the same direction." Faithfulness over the long haul will produce fruitfulness and fulfillment. Staying the course in mid-life will determine the quality of our future life, leadership, and legacy (as well as our eternal rewards).

Over the years, I have learned that the following five disciplines of faithfulness have helped keep me going in my life and leadership (especially during the difficult seasons). Although these five disciplines are not mandatory for everyone, they do address the weaknesses and vulnerabilities in my life. My disciplines of faithfulness include:

1. Goal setting

2. Self-evaluation

3. Spiritual disciplines

4. Commitment to marriage/family

5. Recreation

You might come up with a slightly different list. That is OK as long as they are Biblical and lead you to become more like Christ. But to have no or a "foggy" understanding of disciplines of faithfulness by the time you reach mid-life is dangerous and an invitation to burnout, blowout, or plateauing.

1. **Goal Setting** - I am not a natural goal oriented person. I am idealistic, impulsive, easily distracted, and highly relational. I have good ideas (occasionally even a "GOD" idea), but get bored with details and maintenance after implementation. In my younger years, I was able to accomplish a lot of stuff through will power and hard work, but my life was not especially purposeful. I kind of took the machine gun approach - "if you fire enough shots you are bound to hit the target."

It was not until my 40's that I began to transition from the machine gun approach to the marksman approach. Through the influence of J. Robert (Bobby) Clinton I became aware of the concept of "focused living." In Chapter 8: Moving Towards Focus, Richard will describe this concept and process in greater detail. Let me explain this concept briefly here because it relates significantly to my growth in understanding my calling and how to cooperate with God in preparation for its fulfillment.

Clinton defines the focused life as "a life dedicated to exclusively carrying out God's unique purpose... by identifying the focal issues of life purpose, major role, effective methodology, or ultimate contribution, which allows an increasing prioritization of life's activities around focal issues... resulting in a satisfying life of being and doing" (*Clinton's Biblical Leadership Commentary*, p. 403). Clinton (p. 404-405) describes four components of the focused life:

1. **Life purpose(s)** – "a burden-like calling, a task or driving force or achievement, which motivates a leader to fulfill something or to see something done." (p. 403)

2. **Major role** – "the official or unofficial position, or status/platform or leadership functions, or job description which basically describes what a leader does and which allows recognition by others and which uniquely fits who a leader is and lets that leader effectively accomplish life purpose(s)." (p. 403-404)

3. **Effective methodology** – "ministry insight(s) around which the leader can [effectively] pass on to others the essentials of [life purpose]..." (p. 404)

4. **Ultimate contribution(s)** – "a lasting legacy... for which [the leader] is remembered and which furthers the cause of Christianity by one or more of the following:

    a. Setting standards for life and ministry,
    b. Impacting lives [through evangelism and/or disciple-making],
    c. Serving as a stimulus for change which betters the world,
    d. Leaving behind an organization, institution, or movement that will further... God's work,
    e. Discovery of ideas, communication of them, or promotion of them so that they further God's work."

Clinton (p. 404-405) goes on to describe twelve general ultimate contribution categories that a given leader can leave behind as a legacy to the next generation(s). They include:

- Saint – model life
- Stylistic practitioner – model ministry
- Mentor – personal ministry
- Public rhetorician – public oratory ministry
- Pioneer – opens new types of ministry
- Change agent – helps correct things
- Artist – creative breakthroughs in ministry
- Founder – begins an organization
- Stabilizer – improves an organization
- Researcher – explores things for concepts underlying them
- Writer – produces literature about ideas researched
- Promoter – motivates people to use things and do things

This concept of focused living challenged me to begin to prayerfully try to understand the issues of life purpose, major role, effective methodology, and ultimate contributions. Over the years I have gradually gained valuable insight in each of these areas. Goal setting in the context of an accountable mentoring relationship with Bobby has helped me greatly to develop focus and maintain faithfulness over the long haul. Beginning in 1991 (through 1999), Bobby helped me establish a goal setting strategy around the following principles:

- Goals need to be established out of "hearing and obedience" motivation through prayer and Bible study.

- Goals need to be written, realistic, and measurable.

- Someone needs to hold you accountable.

- Goals need to be evaluated periodically and adjusted if necessary.

Bobby helped me develop a grid for establishing my yearly goals around the general headings of personal development, Bible study, research, and personal ministry using the ultimate contribution(s) categories. Here are my written goals for one of the years he worked with me:

Verse for Year: "Entrust to faithful men, who will be able to teach others..." (II Timothy 2: 2, NIV)

Headings/ Categories	Goal	Activities
1. Personal Development (MARRIAGE)	Develop partnership with Leslie	1. daily prayer for marriage 2. help w/ housework, home schooling, children 3. regular (2 times/week) walks 4. lunch together (at least once/every other month) 5. include in ministry (at least 1 outreach, conference/year)

2. Personal Development (FAMILY)	Disciple Sarah, Matt, and Anna	1. regular (2 times/week) play 2. daily prayer for children 3. include in ministry (at least 1 outreach, conference/year)
3. Personal Development (SAINT)	Deepen devotional life	1. daily prayer (intimacy w/ God) 2. directed fasting (intercession) 3. read through NT 2-3 times
4. Bible Study (SAINT)	Leadership lessons	1. study issues related to mid-life 2. study issues related to reaching and training the next generation
5. Research (SAINT/ MENTOR)	Mid-Life ministry Next Generation	1. continue to collect research (for writing *Living and Leading Well*) 2. continue to collect research for mentoring the next generation of leaders
6. Personal Ministry (PROMOTER/ MENTOR)	Leader development	1. develop written strategy for OBC (identification, training, deployment, and support)

7. Personal Ministry (TEACHER/ MENTOR)	Teaching/ mentoring	1. further develop teaching gift (philosophy, style, technique) 2. continue upward mentoring w/ Bobby (distant) and Dan 3. continue lateral mentoring w/ Richard, Rick, and Ken 4. develop lateral mentoring with Dave and Trent 5. establish downward mentoring w/ students (2 small groups)

Once my goals were written, I would monitor them weekly and submit written monthly updates to Bobby. Occasionally I would talk with Bobby on the phone or visit, but the responsibility to accomplish these goals was mine. At the end of each year I would rate whether I was consistent (+), irregular (/), or did not accomplish (-) my goals. Usually I was consistent on about two-thirds of my goals and usually I set too many goals or unrealistic goals.

Prior to setting goals for the next year, I would prayerfully evaluate my last year and make decisions about whether to continue specific goals, adjust other goals, or abandon some of my past goals.

Although I do not currently goal set in the way I did throughout the 90s, I continue to establish yearly goals through a personal strategic planning grid (for more information on this see the Resource section, *The Extraordinary Power of a Focused Life*). Having done this throughout the 90s has greatly helped me to gain self-discipline and focus.

Also, over time I began to gain a clearer sense of who I was becoming and what God's purpose for me is. This is what I know about focused living for myself at this point in my life:

1. **Life purpose(s)** – I am called to identify, train, deploy, and support leaders (especially young emerging leaders) for the church and the soon coming harvest.

2. **Major role** – I am to resource individuals and teams for finishing well through writing, teaching, mentoring, consulting, coaching, and piloting new leadership training models.

3. **Effective methodology** – I am to accomplish God's calling as part of a team using my primary spiritual gifts of teaching, prophecy, and leadership to empower leaders (especially young emerging leaders) through casting vision, writing, discovery learning training, and mentoring>empowering> multiplication (M>E>M).

4. **Ultimate contribution(s)** – My ultimate contributions (if I finish well and I am committed to doing so by God's grace) will probably be as mentor, change agent, writer, and promoter. My sense is that my most important contribution will be investing in younger emerging leaders.

Knowing these things helps me to be more focused as long as I remain accountable and regularly evaluate myself prayerfully. I have a pretty clear sense of who I am and what God wants me to do. Consequently, I am more strategic and intentional about the decisions I make.

2. **Self-Evaluation** - It is so easy to get caught up in the momentum of life. There seems to be plenty of drama to go around, so taking time for self-evaluation or "self-leadership" will have to be scheduled in or it will not happen.

I try to schedule times of self-evaluation at least quarterly with a mandatory year-end evaluation and goal setting time. My self-evaluation times include prayerfully updating my personal timeline and life and leadership lessons, examination of issues related to character growth, evaluation of my calendar and check book to see if my behavior is consistent with my life purpose and core values, evaluation of progress on my ministry goals, and evaluation of my travel schedule and how it impacts my wife and family. One exercise in self-evaluation that I have found especially helpful is to prayerfully examine my life in relationship to the characteristics of an overseer ("elder") as described in the Bible. These characteristics are:

Characteristics of Overseers and Elders - I Timothy 3: 2-7/ Titus 1: 6-9 (headings from J. Oswald Sanders' *Spiritual Leadership*, p. 39-45)

1. **Social** –
   * "above reproach"
   * "good reputation with outsiders"

2. **Moral** –
   * "blameless"
   * "loves what is good"
   * "temperate... not given to drunkenness"
   * "self-controlled"

3. **Mental** –
   * "able to teach"
   * "encourage others by sound doctrine"
   * "refute those who oppose [sound doctrine]"

4. **Personal** –
   * "gentle, not quarrelsome"
   * "not overbearing"
   * "not a lover of money"
   * "hospitable"

5. **Domestic –**
   * "husband of but one wife"
   * "manage his own family well"
   * "see that his children obey him with proper respect"

6. **Maturity –**
   * "must not be a recent convert"

None of us will have all of these characteristics perfectly, but if we aspire to Christian leadership we will need to experience them substantially. We need to be growing in these areas. An honest assessment of where we are in these areas can lead to growth and transformation. I have developed five self-assessment forms for this process of self-evaluation leading to growth and transformation for mid-life leaders. They include:

* Love Inventory – Appendix A
* Burnout Inventory – Appendix B
* Blowout Inventory – Appendix C
* Plateauing Inventory – Appendix D
* Accountability Inventory – Appendix E

These inventories can be used individually and in accountability relationships with a trusted mentor. The first form is Biblically based and the others are experientially based. Prayerful and careful personal assessment using these inventories can lead to growth and transformation as we move through mid-life and prepare to finish well.

3. **Spiritual Disciplines** - The development of a consistent devotional life has not come easy for me. Early on I tried several approaches to establishing a quiet time but was not able to follow through consistently or failed miserably. Because I am a pretty performance oriented person, I can easily come under condemnation, discouragement, self-pity, and depression if I am not careful. The antidote to performance orientation is grace - an understanding

that I am loved, valued, and accepted by God. Learning to live in a grace-oriented relationship with God and others has helped me tremendously in learning how to appropriate the spiritual disciplines necessary for growth and transformation.

I have read extensively over the years in the areas of spiritual formation, discipleship, and classic spiritual disciplines. The one book that I keep coming back to (besides the Bible) is Richard Foster's *Celebration of Discipline.* Foster's definition of the classical spiritual disciplines and his outline of disciplines has been especially helpful for me. Foster describes the disciplines as "disciplines of grace." He describes these disciplines in three primary categories of four each:

Inward Disciplines:
* Meditation
* Prayer
* Fasting
* Study

Outward Disciplines:
* Simplicity
* Solitude
* Submission
* Service

Corporate Disciplines:
* Confession
* Worship
* Guidance
* Celebration

I have discovered over the years that regular Bible study, meditation, prayer (and fasting), and solitude have become major doors for inner transformation and periodic times of refreshing in my life. I do not necessarily do all of them every day, but they have become regular practices in my life.

Each of us must find our own practice of the spiritual disciplines if we want to live and lead well. We are all different. We have different personalities, gifts, and experiences. There is creativity and celebration in finding which disciplines work for us. The bottom line is that we must find what works for us and regularly incorporate these spiritual disciplines into our lives.

Periodic times of evaluation can help keep us on track in this area. I try to take a day of reflection every six months. During this time I try to prayerfully update my time-line and leadership lessons and ask God to evaluate me in terms of my relationships, schedule, and ministry effectiveness. I also try to remain open to God along the way and keep short accounts of my sin (I John 1: 9) so that I can live and lead with a clear conscience and without unresolved issues.

4. **Commitment to Marriage and Family** - As I mentioned in Chapter 2: Mid-Life Challenges, I have had a difficult time "getting it" as a husband and father. I have always wanted to be a good husband and father and I had great parents who modeled loving commitment to each other and graciousness (and a lot of patience) toward me. I have even read most of the "how I did it" books on marriage and family.

The fact is that I did not understand experientially what it meant to be a good husband and father. Because of my performance orientation, I needed to accomplish stuff (especially in the ministry realm) to feel good about myself. Often in my marriage and family life I have been aware of my limitations that made me feel even more insecure and in need of a performance fix.

Do not misunderstand me here; I have a great wife and wonderful children. My problems in being a good husband and father were and are my problems (not someone else's)! And this understanding is why commitment to my marriage and family has become a discipline of faithfulness (and devotion) for me. I have learned that I have to work at (through grace) being a good husband and father.

I developed a personal checklist that helped me grow in this area:

* Regular dates with my wife – at least once per month
* Regular connection times with my wife (usually in the evening) – at least three times per week
* One-on-one times with the kids (usually a meal out) – at least once a month
* Attend kids activities regularly (depending on travel schedule)
* Celebrate (some spontaneously) successes, breakthroughs, birthdays, anniversaries, holidays as a family
* Family outings and vacations – one big one each year

Up until the last few years, I traveled quite a bit as part of my role as leadership development leader for an association of churches, so I included my wife in helping me manage my travel calendar. We established some general parameters that included no more than 10 nights a month away from home and no more than two weekends a month away from home.

I have found that a general checklist like this is best for me over time as roles and responsibilities change. Life was different when all three of our kids lived at home. As we approached the empty nest transition, my wife asked me not to travel as much. We negotiated the parameters and have come up with a mutually beneficial arrangement. We both work part time, I travel only 1-2 times quarterly, and we are enjoying our life together as we mutually support each other in areas of giftedness and calling.

The specifics of this checklist and how it works out has changed, but having a checklist has helped me be more focused and accountable in these important areas. The bottom line for me is that I have had to learn to become less selfish in order to become a better husband and father. I am still in process, but I am growing and with the growth have come the fulfillment that only a healthy marriage and family can give.

5. **Recreation** - "All work and no play" is an invitation to burnout, blowout, or plateauing. In order to live and lead well we need to develop a healthy and balanced life. We are to love God with all our heart, soul, and mind (Matthew 22: 37), not just in one area of our being.

Psalms 37: 4 states that we are to "delight" ourselves in God and that he will give us "the desires of our heart." Delight and desires speaks of joy and enjoyment, not just duty and hard work. Do not misunderstand me, much of life involves duty and hard work, but a healthy, balanced life also involves delight and the development of our God-given desires.

Recreation speaks of a "re-creating" or renewal process that can help us stay healthy and balanced. The concept of Sabbath rest in the Old Testament (Genesis 2: 2) and of abiding rest of the New Testament (Hebrews 4: 1-13) suggest that there is a healthy rhythm of work and rest that can be enjoyed.

For me, I have cultivated a couple of non-work or recreational interests over the years. They are tennis and fly-fishing. Both can have a competitive or performance orientation so I have had to learn not to work at my recreation. I am in process with both as I like winning better than loosing and I like catching fish better than getting "skunked." But over time I am learning how to enjoy hitting the ball well (a relative concept) and casting a fly well in beautiful surroundings. Both have helped me get and stay balanced and have become activities that I can share with family and friends.

Playing tennis and fly-fishing are not the point, but serve as means to gain exercise, solitude, and a different perspective. You may not be interested in tennis or fly-fishing. That is OK, but if you are in mid-life and do not have any healthy outlets from work you may be out of balance and headed for trouble. Remember, some day you will probably retire from your position and transition to whatever is next. Will you know what to do with your time; will you have developed relationships beyond work; do you and your wife have some activities that you both can enjoy?

My five disciplines of faithfulness are not comprehensive by any means. They are the areas that I sense God has led me to prioritize in my life over the years. The consistent practice of them has aided in God's maturing and transformation process and helped me live and lead well so that I will be prepared to finish well.

Critical in the development and application of these disciplines in my life has been the influence and empowering of mentors. We all need others in our lives. Without them we are lonely and without necessary resources for healthy living and ministry. In Chapter 11: Accountability and Mentoring, I will talk more about this. But before that, Richard will share with you about enhancements that can help prepare you for finishing well and leaving a lasting legacy.

Evaluation and Application

1. What are the five disciplines of faithfulness? What do you think of them? What disciplines would you delete or add to your own list?

2. Do you have a strategy for remaining faithful? If so, what is it and how are you doing? If not, what do you need to do to start developing one and when do you plan to have your plan in place?

3. What is your overall assessment of your life and leadership (based on the five assessments)? What are you doing well? What areas do you need to develop and how are you going to address these areas?

4. Are you accountable to anybody? If so, who is it and how does this person hold you accountable? If not, what is your plan to get real accountability in your life and when do you plan to begin?

Chapter 8

Moving Towards Focus

Would you like a wake-up call? Anyone remember wake-up calls? In the summer of 2008, I received a significant wake up call. But it was not a wake-up call that I asked for, and in fact, I wasn't even aware that I needed to wake up. It was a call from God.

Wake-up… Get Focused!

One morning I was riding my bicycle to work. It was about a 45-minute ride that I really enjoyed. I was riding along and listening to a sermon from one of my favorite preachers. I was going down a hill at a pretty fast pace when all of a sudden a big dump truck made a left turn onto the bike path I was on. The driver did not see me. Suddenly, the truck was right in front of me. I had about one second to react and I knew in that moment that there was nothing I could do. I could not avoid hitting that truck. And hit the truck I did!

In the next moment, I found myself on the ground looking up at the sky. The first thing that I realized was that I was not dead. In fact, after a quick survey, I realized that I did not seem to have any life threatening injuries. I said a quick prayer of thanks! Then I noticed that my bike had been crushed underneath the truck's tires. The police arrived shortly after and were making comments like, "You are lucky to be alive!" The ambulance drivers checked me out and said, "We can't believe that you don't have more things wrong with you. We are taking you to the hospital to check you out." At the hospital, all the doctors, nurses, and X-ray technicians kept saying the same things, "We can't believe that you aren't more injured."

During the lengthy process of checking everything out, I had time to think and reflect on what had just happened. At one point, while alone on a hospital bed waiting for the next test to be done, my mind heard the familiar quiet voice that I love to hear.

"Richard?"

"Yes, Lord."

"It could have been over today."

"Yes, Lord, I am just now beginning to realize that. You rescued me didn't you?"

"Yes, I did. I pulled you off that bike when it went under the truck. Why do you think I did that?"

"You love me and my family."

"Yes that is true but there is more. There is more for you to do in this life. Wake up. Get focused."

That was it. Four words... "Wake up. Get focused!" In that moment, I had a profound sense of God's love and felt surrounded by his protection. I also found that something deep inside of me was responding to God, something that I had not even been conscious of.

I walked away from the accident with damaged shoulders, a dislocated right thumb, and lots of aches and pains. God's healing power touched me in a miraculous way, but it did take some time. Over the following six weeks, I had lots of time to reflect and pray as I healed from the injuries.

This experience was the motivation that I needed to start making some adjustments in my life. It provided some much needed motivation to do some evaluation and reflection about my own leadership development. Just one month earlier, I had been together with my father, my friend Paul Leavenworth, and Terry Walling. We were talking about what happens to leaders in the middle stages of their development. At that time I had made some inner commitments to God that I would make some changes. I knew that I needed to make what my friend Paul will call "some mid-course corrections" in my journey with God.

As we write this book, Paul and I are aware that many of you who are reading this book need a wake-up call as well. Naturally, I pray that you can experience a less dramatic and painful one than I received. As I interacted with God during my recovery time, I realized that God had brought me to a moment of decision. It was not a moment of decision that comes because of external circumstances. It was an internal decision. It was a decision that very few people around me even knew that I needed to make. They were unaware of the growing turmoil within me. Other than my wife, no one knew that I was reaching a critical point on the inside. But I knew. I knew that I was approaching a strategic moment.

Decision Making: Which Way Do I Go?

In the course of a leader's development, every one of us will come to face many strategic and critical moments in the journey. I am not thinking about the moments where we decide whether to sin or not. That choice is always clear. God wants us to turn to him and resist the temptation to make a sinful choice. I am talking about those moments in life where we make decisions that shape the journey we are on.

At these strategic moments, we will need to make decisions. Sometimes the decisions are visible and can be dramatic. The road we are driving on comes to an end and we have to make a choice: left or right? These are two very different options, each going in different directions. For example, our sense of calling to move from the United States to Switzerland was one of those decisions. In many ways, I was doing the same things in the U.S. that I would be doing anywhere else in the world, but the road we were on had come to an end. We had to choose: left or right? We do not face these kinds of decisions every year. These are the big ones. These are the types of critical decisions we face during times of transition.

Becoming Focused

There are other situations where we face critical decisions that are strategic, but not so visible. They have to do with what we call "becoming focused." In the special leadership language we have developed (Clintonese), we call this "focused living." It simply means that we are making decisions to cooperate with God that line up with who God has designed us to be and what he has created us to do.

One of the most strategic decision making processes that we go through in the middle stages of leadership development is learning when to say "Yes" and when to say "No." Of course, this means that we really need to know what to say yes to and what we should say no to.

Assuming that we are not talking about sinful choices, all of the yes options are good ones and all of the no options are also good things. Before my accident, none of the things that I was doing were bad things. In fact, they were all good things. I was sharing the love of God with people and I was involved in serving them and investing in the Kingdom of God. What I was doing was not wrong, but many of those things were keeping me from saying yes to other things. It was like looking at a menu at your favorite restaurant. All the choices are good and you really cannot make a bad decision but the meals can be quite different from one another.

Another metaphor may help here. It would be like playing golf without putting my contact lenses in. I need them for distant vision. Without them I could still hit the ball. I could still see the course. I could still enjoy the surroundings. But my golfing would be a significantly different experience. I would spend most of my time looking for my ball. I would know the basic direction that I hit the ball in. I might even be able to guess about how far I hit it. The closer shots would not be as difficult, but the longer shots would be more difficult. I could imagine myself saying, "Oh, I didn't see that hazard from the tee." "If I would have seen that, I would have made a different choice about which club to hit." Those of you that play golf know what I am talking about.

God Has a Specific Plan

In all the books in the Well Trilogy, we have been working with the basic assumption that God is sovereign and that he has created each one of us in a unique way. He has a plan for our lives. He has created us to accomplish specific purposes that he has been shaping us to do. In the middle stages of development, we have reached the season of development where we should be increasingly aware of the specific details of God's plan for our lives. What was general before now begins to become more specific. God's vision for our life, our life experiences, our values, our giftedness, our opportunities and our leadership experiences are increasingly moving us into greater and greater focus.

We believe that God is deliberately and intentionally developing leaders for their full potential. Potential can be measured in many ways. But without getting too technical, a person's potential is reached when their character is mature and they are operating at full efficiency and effectiveness. Another way of saying this is: we believe that God wants each leader to be in the right place, doing the right things, in the way that best fits the way God has designed them. If this is God's plan, then it leads to several other questions:

1. **How does a leader know what their potential is?** Ultimately, God can only know the answer to this question. Our understanding of the answer to this question can only come from our experience with God. This is a discovery process. High ego strength individuals will think that they have much more potential than low ego strength individuals.

In my own experience, these are the assumptions that I use to answering this question about potential:

1. God knows what my potential is.
2. He is developing me to fulfill my potential.
3. My job is not to identify or figure out exactly what my potential is.
4. My job is to respond to what God is doing with me.
5. I am to pursue learning, growing, and developing.
6. I am to obey him when he tells me to do something.

At the end of the day, if I act on these assumptions, I will have reached my potential. In heaven, I will be able to see how I did when

God helps me to look back over my life with his perspective. In the meantime, I just keep trying to grow more mature in my character, keep learning to enhance the skills that I have, and I stay open to growing by embracing the new challenges that he brings my way. I try not to worry about what my potential is. I have learned that the truth about potential is this: If we are consistently obedient over the long haul we will realize our potential.

2. **What if my cultural context limits my ability to make decisions?** Having the freedom to make whatever individual choices we want is not always possible. In the Western world, we consider it our right to do this, but in many cultures and situations, leaders are not as free to make choices like this. A leader's ability to choose is severely limited by contextual factors over which they have little or no control. In many cultures, making an individual choice would never be considered. Decisions are made through group processes.

But having said this, God is sovereign and even in these situations he still calls individuals to obediently follow him. Although the process may seem very different and the way choices are made may be different, God calls individuals to follow him regardless of their circumstances. The stories of the leaders in the Bible are stories about leaders who lived in non-Western cultures and these leaders made individual choices often in extremely difficult circumstances.

The biblical character Daniel was one of those leaders who had very little freedom to make personal decisions. From the time he was a teenager until he was an old man, many of his life decisions were made for him. The decisions Daniel made were mostly internal and made under great peril. That is what makes his internal decisions to follow Yahweh so dramatic. His example leads me to believe that God can lead an individual toward focus no matter what their circumstances are or whatever culture they live in.

With this in mind, I want to focus in on the issues that help us to find clarity. We want to move towards clarity... clarity in our vision, clarity in our values that shape our ministry philosophy, clarity in our understanding of our giftedness, and clarity in the leadership roles that we have. In this chapter, I will focus on clarity in relationship to vision. In the following chapters (9 and 10), I will focus on clarity as it relates to values, ministry philosophy, and ministry roles.

Without Vision People...

Recently I was working on understanding the spiritual principle that is communicated in Proverbs 29:18 which I first learned in the King James Version. It says, "Where there is no vision, people perish." When I looked it up in a Hebrew literal translation, I found that the Hebrew word translated "perish" in the literal Hebrew is "made naked." Without a "vision" people are "made naked"

I began to read various ways that the interpreters have translated this verse. For the Hebrew word "vision", I found the various translations included words like vision, revelation, message from God, divine guidance, no understanding of the Word of the Lord, can't see what God is doing.

Add this to the Hebrew "made naked" and the interpreters came up with:

> "People perish, people have no restraint, people don't control themselves, people run wild, people do whatever they want."

One thing is really clear, no matter how you translate these key words: We need to know what God is communicating to us. We need direction, vision from God. What happens to people when they do not have Godly vision is not an option that anyone wants. This is even more important for leaders. Not only do we need to hear from God for ourselves, we have the responsibility of hearing from God for the group that we are leading.

I remember hearing John Maxwell say in a conference, "Show me a leader without vision and I'll show you someone who isn't going anywhere. At best, he/she is traveling in circles." I think this is what Proverbs 29:18 is saying as it is applies to the leadership process. Tom Marshall, *Understanding Leadership*, makes this point very clear when he writes:

> "If leaders are not aiming at something and are merely responding or reacting to situations as they arise, they have already virtually surrendered leadership. If circumstances are determining what is going to be done, then the role of the leader has become one of maintenance because the attention is focused on the present or the past rather than on the future." (p. 9-10)

I believe that it is this lack of clarity about vision that leads to so many leadership problems in the middle stages of our leadership development. This is as true of our personal vision of ourselves as it is of our leadership with the groups God has called us to serve.

George Barna, *Leaders on Leadership* (editor), defines vision as "a clear mental portrait of a preferable future, communicated by God to His chosen servant-leaders, based upon an accurate understanding of God, self, and circumstances" (p. 47).

We have already shared in our Introduction the definition of a leader that J. Robert Clinton wrote in his book, *The Making of a Leader*. From his definition, one could say that, "vision is the description of God's purposes communicated to the leader in advance for the group they are leading."

Vision Under Attack!

Most of us do not like to think about or focus on spiritual warfare but that does not change the reality that we are under attack. I believe that leaders are under specific attack from the enemy in the area of vision. The enemies of God will do everything possible to block God's vision from coming to the leader. If they cannot block it, they want to reduce the leader's capacity to get vision from God by distracting them or diluting the vision to make it as unclear as possible. I believe that this is especially true for leaders who are coming into the middle stages of life and leadership development.

I had an interesting experience a few years ago that reminded me of this kind of spiritual warfare. Spiritual warfare is a reality and we have to learn to fight effectively, but it is not something that I think about all the time. I was in some leadership meetings in California with my father and some other leaders. We were together for a week. On the first day I was wrestling on the inside with the contrast between the cultural differences between leadership meetings in my ministry context in Europe and this leadership setting. The atmosphere was so different. The way the leaders spoke about their visions, their ministries, their dreams, and their leadership was so different from what I had been accustomed to in Europe. Everything seemed possible. There was a kind of optimistic faith when people spoke about the future.

After being with them for five days, something in me started to change. In fact, I started to dream, reflect, and talk to God in a different way. And I believed that God started to speak to me. In fact, I wrote down some specific things that I believed that God said to me. It concerned some ideas about new things to do. It was vision! I could see it. I could feel it. I could imagine it. I could believe it.

Then I flew home to Europe. I looked at the things I had written down and wondered... "Was that really God?" The day after I arrived home, I was organizing my computer files and working to follow up on the things that needed to be done. When I came to the vision that I had written down, I though, "Well that was a nice idea but... I will have to pray about it." A few days later, I was sharing with the leaders in my church about what God had done while we were in the U.S. When I got to the part about the vision, I thought, "I don't even want to mention it." When I looked at the leaders faces, I thought, "No one has any energy to try another new thing. I better not burden them with another new idea." Gone! The vision was gone. I could not see it. I could not feel it. I could not imagine it. I could not believe it.

A week later I shared this experience with another American who had lived in Switzerland for a long time. Her comment was, "Yes, the spiritual warfare is really strong here, isn't it?" Suddenly, I realized what had happened. She was right. Vision was under attack. And I had just been assigning this activity to "cultural differences."

Leaders without God's vision will not be effective in God's kingdom. It seems evident that this is part of the ongoing warfare that we are engaged in. Learning how to put on the full armor of God (Ephesians 6) in the midst of these kinds of attacks can help us own God's vision and prepare us to contend for it.

The Parable of the Vision

Here is an interesting exercise that I did after reflecting on this issue. I took the Parable of the Sower and I put the word "vision" in the place of the "seed" which Jesus tells us is God's word. After all, vision from God is a word from God. The parable spoke to me in a fresh way. It was a real challenge to me. Jesus is speaking to his leaders. Listen to how it sounds:

> "Leaders, the seed is a word of vision from God. Some leaders are like the seed that fell along the path. As soon as they hear vision from God, Satan comes and takes it away. Other leaders are like the seed that is thrown on the rocky ground. They hear vision from God and they receive it with joy but they only hold on to the vision for a short time. When the vision is challenged or trouble and persecution comes, the vision dies and the leader falls away from it. Other leaders are like the seed that fell among the thorns. They see the vision from God but

> their anxiety about life and the deceitfulness of wealth and the desire for other things chokes the life out of the vision. The vision doesn't come to pass. However, other leaders receive the vision from God and they are ready to believe it, act on it and obey it. The vision from God will be fulfilled way beyond anything they could imagine." (Clinton paraphrase)

Challenging, isn't it? What kind of "vision soil" are you? What happens to vision when it lands on you? As I am making my way through this journey with God, this goes right to the heart of the issues that block me from staying well, fighting well, or running well. What do I really believe about God? What is he really like? What do I really believe God has told me to do?

In our leadership studies, we have identified the major barriers that block leaders from finishing well. We have observed issues like problems in the family, the abuse of power, misusing resources, growth that is blocked or stops, and illicit sexual relationships. We have not looked as closely or identified what led leaders to the place where they made the poor decisions or the sinful choices that led them away from God and God's purposes for their lives. But I am convinced that the core of the problem lies in the leader's disconnection with God and failing to see God's vision for their lives in a clear way. When God's vision becomes unclear, it is impossible to live and lead well or to stay on track.

Things That Attack Vision Clarity

Here are some of the common attacks against a leader's vision. They are all related to one another and they all have one goal: visionary distortion and blindness.

1. **Who is in control?** In the gospel of John, God uses the word "cosmos" which is most often translated in English "the world."

Recently I was listening to some sermons by Darrell Johnson who is a professor at Regent Seminary in Vancouver, BC. He points out that John uses this term "cosmos" to describe "humanity organized without reference to God." The world, according to John, is the result of what happens when humanity tries to live without God. The world is structured to eliminate God. Philosophy, knowledge, government, religious systems, the arts and media are all systems that are being used to organize our world under the control of the one who Jesus calls "the prince of this world".

The enemy uses every means possible to get people to take their eyes off of God and to put their eyes on something else. When our eyes are looking at something or someone other than God, our vision weakens. And this "world system" is bombarding us with images that are not coming from God. These images are designed to make us focus on something other than God's vision.

Antidote: The author of Hebrews points out this danger at the beginning of chapter 12. After writing the wonderful chapter on faith, the writer exhorts us to fix our eyes on Jesus. Not just looking at Jesus, but learning to see through Jesus' eyes. How does Jesus see what is happening around us? How does Jesus look at our lives, our future, our dreams, or our desires? How does Jesus see the ministry we are involved in or the church we are working in? What is he looking at and what is he seeing? By focusing on this, our vision becomes clearer.

The ultimate clarity comes when we can see the big picture. Reading through the last book in the Bible is all about having a clear picture of the big picture. And our vision becomes most clear when we look into heaven and we see that the throne is occupied. In Revelation 4, we are told that the Lamb of God sits on the throne. When we see this clearly, we have the possibility of seeing everything else more clearly.

2. **Watch out for the danger of pessimism and negativity!** One of the natural tendencies for leaders who are in mid-life is to become somewhat pessimistic or negative. Much of the cultural

data around us is telling us that the world is out of control. Many of our own hurtful or damaging experiences in the past are telling us to become less trusting and more realistic. All of this can contribute to a tendency of having an attitude of, "been there, tried that, didn't work." Some personality types are more in danger of this trap than others, but even the most optimistic and positive personalities have to watch out.

Living and leading well and staying on track involve maintaining the right levels of optimism. The key to this is connected to where we choose to focus our attention.

"Is the glass half full or half empty?" " Where do we focus?" I heard a pastor recently talk about how his church leadership had set the goal of seeing a specific number of new converts over a certain period of time. In his context, seeing people move through the process of conversion is usually quite slow and to be honest, the spiritual soil is quite hard and resistant. His number sounded very ambitious to all of the other pastors listening. However, he reported that God had exceeded that number and God had done even more than they expected. What a positive report! The next sentence out of the pastor's mouth was, "But it could have even been better. There could have been much more." How tragic! A moment to celebrate was lost. A positive situation turned into something less positive. We need to watch out.

Antidote: First, we can guard against this danger by recognizing and admitting that there is potential danger. Unmet goals and disappointments are a natural part of gaining life and leadership experience. What we do with disappointments, seemingly unfulfilled prayers, missed targets, criticisms, hurts and all the other things that can happen to a leader is the critical issue. How do we process all of this? Will we find healthy and God pleasing ways to process what happens to us in a way that does not diminish our faith and our confidence in God? This is easier said than done.

Secondly, we must work very hard to learn how God evaluates and what God determines is important. Most of the time when I experience myself getting negative or pessimistic, it happens because I am looking at the situation differently than God is. When God lifts me out of negativity and pessimism (which has happened more than I like to admit), he usually does it by making an adjustment with my vision. He shows me how to look at the situation from his perspective and he opens my eyes to see it. I often need to ask myself these two questions: What does God measure? How does God measure?

Thirdly, I need to consistently work on accepting the sovereignty of God. I need to strengthen my faith and stay focused on the fact that he is in control! A friend of mine used to put the following phrase at the bottom of every email, "God is in control and he never makes a mistake." I like the sound of that. I actually believe that, but it does not always 'feel' true. Another friend of mine used to say a phrase that I have repeated thousands of times. He would say in response to something that was going wrong or some new challenge, "Don't worry. There's no panic in heaven!" I just love that. It brings me back to a place where I choose to believe again in God's sovereignty and this reinforces my resolve to stay away from negativity and pessimism.

Fourthly, I need to anchor myself to the things that do not change such as God's heart for the world, God's character, and God's Word. I find that the very best thing that I can do to avoid becoming negative or pessimistic is to immerse myself in the Bible and spend time in God's presence. I do not go into the Bible or into his presence to get answers or get my problems solved. I do it just to be with him and focus on what he has revealed about himself. This can bring perspective and hope - things that anchor me.

3. **Loss of courage (unwillingness to take risks)**. I have read the first chapter of Joshua many times. "Be strong and have courage." That is the phrase that always leaps off the page at me. The fact that God spoke this to Joshua points out that leaders have options when they face big challenges. Being weak and losing courage is one of them. If I am honest with myself, I must admit that I have felt this option. Being weak and losing courage is a default position for many leaders. To move to the "strong and courageous"

option is not something that is automatic. We have to choose it and learn to endure in it.

How do you know if you have courage or not? One of the signals that I have lost courage is that I am less willing to take risks. In general, the older I get the less willing I am to take risks. Some of this is for good reasons. Maybe it is because I am much more aware of the possible consequences of a decision. I have experienced what happens when a risk is rewarded and I have experienced what happens when taking a risk does not work out. These experiences eat away at my confidence and courage. We are not called to take risks without measuring, evaluating, or being ready for the consequences. Jesus told us that we should be very wise in counting the cost before we take a risk. But at the same time, there are situations where we have counted the cost and we face a moment of decision. Do we go for it or not? Clarity of vision is the key factor here. What is God up to and what does he want me to do?

The loss of courage affects our vision. This is what happened to the twelve spies who were sent to explore the Promised Land. They started out strong and courageous, but they could not pull the trigger when it came to the moment of decision. What happened? They lost their vision. They took their eyes off of God and put them on the walled cities and the giants. Joshua observed this firsthand and maybe that is why God told him in Joshua 1, "Be strong and have courage." Joshua knew that anything other than a God centered, God focused vision was not going to work.

Antidote: Courage is connected to trust. Without trust, it is impossible or even foolhardy to have courage. To have courage we have to focus ourselves on whom or what we put our trust in. Is our trust focused on us (our strength, our abilities, our resources)? Or is our trust focused on God (his strength, his abilities, his resources)?

My grandmother was a woman of courage. She often used to quote Proverbs 3:5-6, "Trust in the Lord with all your heart and lean not on your own understanding; in all your ways acknowledge him, and he will make your paths straight" (NIV). When I need courage and I need to focus my trust back onto God, I return to these verses and to the promises of God in them. I have to remind myself that I need to trust him and not myself. This refocus rebuilds my confidence and trust in God. Then the courage returns and my willingness to take his risks begin to grow.

4. **Fear.** I think most of us know how fear attacks our vision. When fear suddenly pops up, we naturally respond by closing our eyes. "Out of sight, out of mind!" For me it is usually flinch and close my eyes. Sometimes it is a flinch, gasp, and close my eyes. I believe that we do the same thing in the spiritual realm when we get afraid - we close our eyes. We can no longer see what God sees. Fear attacks our vision.

Antidote: John writes in 1 John 4:18 that perfect love casts out fear. Being in the presence of God's love keeps us free from fear. When fear begins to grip us and we begin to close our eyes and lose the clarity of our vision, it is time to draw near to God and experience his loving presence. That is one of the reasons that leaders need to be connected to a strong community of people. God can share his love by creating an individual encounter with him, but most of the time God works through his community. He reveals himself and his love through his people. That is why it is so dangerous when leaders isolate themselves and do not have a group of people that they can be real with or share life with.

Moving Towards Focus

Moving towards focus begins with finding clarity in our vision: God's vision for the world around us, God's vision for our personal life, and God's vision for the development for our ministry.

Getting a clear vision from God for our lives is a critical step in becoming focused. When we see his plan clearly, we can write it down in a life purpose statement. There are many tools that can help you to write this kind of statement. Having it clear and written down will help a leader to stay on track. It can be added to or changed as God works in our lives, but having a clear personal vision statement can help, especially during the tough times of spiritual attack or personal doubts.

In the next chapter, we will look at some other critical factors that help leaders to move towards focus. We will look at the key issues that relate to a leader developing a unique philosophy of ministry.

Evaluation and Application:

1. What is Godly vision and why is it important for the Christian leader?

2. How does a Godly vision help Christian leaders in their decision-making?

3. How does Godly vision help Christian leaders to gain a clearer sense of life and leadership purpose?

4. What are the primary "attacks" on Godly vision that the Christian leader needs to be aware of?

5. What are the antidotes to these "attacks"? How can you apply them to your life?

6. How are you doing on discovering and being purposeful in fulfilling God's vision and purpose for your life and leadership? What is going right and what changes do you need to make to maximize your purpose?

Chapter 9

Articulating Ministry Philosophy

Have you ever experienced the following? You walk into a setting where you have never been before. For example, imagine going to a church service for the first time. Without conscious thought, something begins to happen inside you as you enter. At first, everything is unfamiliar. You are aware that you are a visitor. Then over the next few minutes, you either start to feel increasingly more comfortable or you feel increasingly more uncomfortable.

What is happening? You are encountering the impact of a ministry philosophy where certain values are being expressed and experienced. Most of the time these values are not written down, although they express a set of convictions and beliefs. These lead to certain behaviors that are expressed through things like the way the room is set up, the way people are treated and greeted, the kind of interaction that is visible, the musical styles, the preaching styles, and the way people pray.

Resonance and Dissonance

Have you ever heard the terms resonance and dissonance? Most of the time, they are used in the context of acoustics. Resonance in acoustics describes the phenomena of what happens to a sound when there is an intensification and prolongation of the sound. Resonance is produced by a sympathetic vibration and results in the amplification or echoing of a sound. The different sounds complement the other sounds.

Dissonance in acoustics describes a combination of sounds that are in discord, a cacophony, or a state of unrest. Dissonant means that there are at least two sounds that are in disagreement, out of harmony, at variance, or incongruous with each other. Dissonance results in an unsettled, conflicting, or even clashing of sounds.

When you walked into the church service, this is what happened to you. You either experienced resonance or dissonance. It happens all the time. All of us have within us a set of values that shape our reactions to what is going on around us. In a ministry setting we call this a ministry philosophy. When the ministry philosophy of the new ministry setting is close to our own, it begins to resonate within us. When the ministry philosophy is not compatible, we begin to experience dissonance.

Ministry Effectiveness and Ministry Philosophy

We have been looking at issues that help leaders stay on track and continue their development during mid-life. My father calls this a "focused life." It begins with a clear vision from God. What has

God said and what is God saying about our destiny? This clear vision from God gives leaders a sense of purpose that helps them move towards accomplishing God's purposes for their lives.

A big part of moving into focus involves making sure that we are in the right ministry setting. There are two issues that are important about the ministry setting: 1. Finding compatibility between a personal ministry philosophy and the ministry philosophy of the organization, and 2. Finding the right ministry role within that organization. In this chapter, I will look at the issue of ministry philosophy. In the next chapter, I will focus on finding the right ministry role.

In order for leaders to move into focus and operate with increasing intentionality and effectiveness, they need to be in ministry settings where their personal ministry philosophy resonates with the philosophy that is operating in the ministry setting.

Resonance or dissonance with a ministry philosophy will determine the freedom that the leader has to move toward effectiveness. We see this dynamic all the time in the sport's world. This dynamic often occurs between coaches and players. In the sport's world this phenomena is described as chemistry. It happens in personal relationships as well. It is one of the intangible factors that affect all of us in leadership and ministry.

Compatibility between a ministry philosophy and an individual's giftedness will also be an influence on a leader's ability to move towards effectiveness. Although giftedness is very important to finding the right ministry role, it also is directly linked to how much freedom the person has to develop and grow. On several occasions, the ministry philosophy of the group I was a part of did not allow the kind of gifts that I was discovering to emerge. The ministry philosophy hindered or even blocked me from using and developing my giftedness. My development got stymied.

Another key issue is having a sense of belonging. In order to move towards effectiveness, leaders need to know that they fit in the group that they are a part of. This sense of belonging allows them the freedom needed to grow. Knowing that you belong is directly linked to the ministry philosophy and values that are being expressed.

For example, how do you know if you belong to a group or not? I once worked with a movement of churches in Switzerland. We were continually looking for people who wanted to join us. But how does one know if they should join or not? How do you know if you are a fit or not?

These are good questions. Our group had not been established for very long so we did not have a clear set of definitions or a clear set of boundaries. We were in the process of developing clarity. So how does one answer questions like these in their group?

I have heard "insiders" say things like, "You know you are in when you feel like you are a part of our family." This is highly subjective and very intuitive. What is meant by the concept of family? The different definitions and experiences of what family means can cause people to experience resonance or dissonance. It all depends on how our internal personal values shape our definitions of family. You can see that we need to be in a process of clarifying and evaluating our values and the values of the ministry philosophy of the group that we are in if we want to experience resonance.

Moving into Focus: Looking for Resonance

In the middle stages of a leader's development, articulating a personal ministry philosophy becomes increasingly important. As the personal ministry philosophy emerges and is discovered, the need to articulate it becomes critical. When it is articulated explicitly, there will be increasing resonance or dissonance with the ministry setting. In the process of articulating the ministry philosophy, compatibility between our personal values and the values and vision of the ministry setting will be much easier to evaluate.

However, this is not an easy process because most of the time, the values are not out in the open. All the action is happening beneath the surface. The values are mostly lodged in the sub-conscious. We are not aware of them. We have picked them up without being aware of them.

There are many excellent books describing how this happens in various cultures around the world. It is a fascinating process. The main point of this chapter is not to explore how values get into us, but rather to bring what is implicit and sub-conscious out into the open and make them more explicit. This is an important task during the middle stages of a leader's development.

Without doing the difficult work of discovering and making our values explicit, it will be very difficult to move ahead in our leadership development. In the early stages of our development, this issue was not as critical. We began in ministry by operating within the ministry philosophy and values that were shaped by other leaders. We simply began to do ministry, growing and learning implicitly by finding out what seems to fit and what does not.

But now in mid-life, it becomes more important. God has designed us to live and lead out of whom he has created us to be. We begin to interact with the values of the ministry setting around us. We have experiences that are disappointing, frustrating, or even painful. We learn who we are not (usually by trying to fit in and be like other leaders around us). We learn what we do not value (usually by going through the pain of rejection or disappointment). But, this is not all bad. At the same time, we have probably experienced some situations and relationships where we found blessing, favor or success. These experiences help us to learn in a positive way who we are and where we fit. This growth process is necessary as we mature and gain greater clarity about who we are and greater focus about what God wants us to do.

Our personal values determine what is important. As our sense of "being" emerges, the issue of resonance or dissonance comes into focus. Without a harmony or resonance between our personal ministry values and the ministry setting, we will find it hard to operate in ministry effectively out of who we are. We will face the reality of being in an increasingly more dissonant working situation and conflicts begin to emerge on a regular basis.

This is called "value dissonance." We are blocked from moving into effectiveness because of the increasing friction between what we think is important and what the ministry setting thinks is important. Consequently, it becomes more and more important to bring our values out into the open while we move toward resonance.

Understanding Ministry Philosophy

In order to understand how a ministry philosophy affects our leadership development, we have to first understand what it is. Then we can understand better how it is developed and how it affects us. The following definitions are based on my father's work on ministry philosophy as well as an excellent book by Edgar Schein called *Organizational Culture and Leadership*. Their work has provided very helpful insights. A ministry philosophy is a set of implicit values. These values influence the leader in three ways:

1. They guide a leader's behavior, thinking, understanding, and ministry styles of his/her ministry.

2. They increasingly help the leader to focus on making the God-given and unique contribution to the kingdom.

3. These values gradually become explicit over a lifetime that allows the leader to pass them on to others and leave a legacy behind.

The Importance of Values

Mostly, values lie underneath a leader's perception and behavior in ministry. They influence how a leader makes decisions, the styles and means that a leader uses to influence followers, and as a means of evaluating ministry.

What exactly is a value? Values are beliefs and expressing values are a part of being human. Values are expressed within the context of every culture, as convictions that help us define what we believe are true about reality. Values shape our understanding of reality and they provide us an explanation of what is important. They help us explain why we do what we do and why we do things the way we do them. Values are the foundation for a ministry philosophy.

Vision describes the "WHAT" while values describe the "WHY." Vision clarifies God's purposes for us or describes what our mission is. Our values give us insight into why we should do what we are doing and they give us insight into how we should go about doing it. This is the essence of a ministry philosophy. Vision and values shape the parameters that we believe are most important. They set specific boundaries for what is important. Values expose or support our motives for why we do things we do. Values provide our motives that manifest in our methods of how we do things.

This is why understanding our values are so important. In order to develop as an effectiveness leader, it is important that we begin to articulate our values and understand how they affect us. I have been mentoring and coaching leaders for a long time and have listened to so many stories involving conflict, pain, misunderstanding, and wounding. In almost every story, what became clear was that the issues involved in the situation revealed the values in the person that were in dissonance.

How Do Values Get Formed in Us?

God uses situations and people to shape our values. By the time we reach mid-life, we have been involved in countless situations and interactions with people. God uses these to shape or form values into us. We learn lessons that help us form opinions or beliefs about what we think is important or what we think is true. We form opinions and beliefs about the right way of doing things. These insights become the basis of our values.

These lessons are blended into our thinking as they happen. We may not be aware of them and how they affect us, but each time that we face a similar experience or situation these lesson about values kick in and help us evaluate the new situation. They tell us how to react, how to respond, and how to evaluate what is happening.

As we continue to accumulate experiences, lessons and values form a grid or foundation of ideas that gives us standards to operate by, guidelines for application, or knowledge for making decisions. Voila! We have a personal ministry philosophy and most of us do not even know it. Most of this learning of values is unconscious as we take in and process values without realizing it.

Clarifying Values

This is why it is so important to do clarifying work. Leaders need to constantly clarify, explain, and evaluate what is meant by the words they use to express their values and behaviors. They need to think through and evaluate why they do what they do and whether it is consistent with what they say they believe. It is critical for mid-life leaders to move our ministry philosophy from being implicit to explicit.

Often it is through conflict situation that leaders have the opportunity to clarify their values. I remember one of the early experiences that I had in a church that I eventually served at in Zurich, Switzerland. Before I agreeing to come and lead the church,

I needed to share and explain what my values were and why they were important to me. Some of the values were core values and some were not as central. I sent these values to the small group that was to become the initial group of the church and we worked through these together. I wanted them to understand how I understood my values and that my vision for any church would flow directly out of my values.

After being in Switzerland for a few months, I ran into a classic "value dissonance" situation. I began to feel a growing sense of dissonance in me. It centered around two of our stated values. When you read these values, you may have a hard time imagining a conflict arising (but it did). They were:

Value 1: We value giving God the best that we have.
Value 2: We value helping people develop their potential.

Both of these values sound good, but I began to realize that these values were being influenced and defined by other stronger values. For example, what did we mean by "best"? In a culture that values excellence but struggles with perfectionism, "best" meant something that I did not want it to mean. Why? Because I found that my value of helping people develop their potential was more important to me than being the "best."

Of course we want to give God our best, but when you are developing your potential, best may not mean "excellence." The reality is that people who are learning and growing do not usually start at excellent. They need time and experience to develop themselves. You can imagine the kind of conflicts that began to emerge.

The ministry context where this value dissonance was very visible was in the worship ministry. Everyone who has ever tried to develop a worship team knows the tension in trying to find the balance between developing people and excellence. When and where do we allow people to participate so they can gain experience and become better at what they do? What is the level of skill and ability that is needed? What does it mean to let them develop?

I discovered that the worship leader had similar sounding values with different meanings. We began to experience dissonance. We needed to clarify what each one of us meant by these values. We either needed to come into harmony with what we meant, change our stated values, or separate before these differences affected our ability to serve others.

Clarifying Exercise

While we are on the topic of worship, let me ask the following questions: "How do you evaluate worship?" "What makes it good and what makes it poor?" Try to articulate your personal worship values. Then ask yourself another couple of questions: "How did I come up with these values?" "Why are these values important to me and the people I serve?"

One of the interesting things for me about traveling around and being in many different kinds of churches is seeing how different churches give meaning to the value of worship. Every church that I have ever been in would list worship as one of the primary activities of their church and it is at or near the top of the list in the things that the church values.

But if you want to do an interesting exercise, ask people a question about their church: "How was the worship last week?" What you will hear is a reflection of their values and you may find them very interesting. I do this quite often and here are some answers that I have heard when I asked the question about last week's worship. I will share only some of the positive answers I have heard:

* "Worship was great … the band was awesome and really put on a great show."
* "Worship was great...14 people gave their lives to Christ."
* "Worship was great.... we had 48 new visitors."
* "Worship was great… the creative team did a fantastic job."

* "Worship was great... we had the biggest offering ever."
* "Worship was great...I have never heard a better sermon."
* "Worship was great... we really set ourselves aside and gave "honor" to God."
* "Worship was great ... I received a prophetic word from ..."
* "Worship was great...I experienced a wonderful touch from God."

If you want to take it a step, you can ask the following question: "How did you 'worship' last week?" Each one of us will focus in on the values that we hold most dearly when asked these types of clarifying questions.

Here are some additional clarifying questions and statements that I have presented to different groups over the years. I instruct people to answer these questions individually by writing their answers in two or three sentences and then encourage them to discuss their answers as a group.

1. "What are the most important things that make a small group really good?"

2. "When God wants to bring healing into a person's life, first God will..."

3. "When someone is having real personal problems, they need to..."

4. "When teaching or preaching, the most important thing is..."

5. "If I want to be effective in prayer, I have to begin by..."

6. "The most important thing about being a leader is ..."

7. "When one of the followers doesn't do something I asked them to do, I need to ..."

8. "The most important things about handling finances in ministry are ..."

9. "If I want to see the financial giving increase in the church, I need to..."

Of course these kinds of clarifying questions could go on and on. You can generate a list of questions or statements like I have listed that will help you to focus in on your personal leadership and ministry values.

Recommendation: Write Out Your Personal Values!

Way back in 1995, I was challenged to do this. I was going through a time of transition and had been reading through my father's *Strategic Concepts* book while doing some leadership reading on ministry philosophy. I decided to try and write out the most important personal and ministry values that I could identify. It took some time, but it was worth it. This growth project proved to be very helpful in many ways. Here are a few things that I learned in the process that may be helpful for you.

At first, I did not really know how to do it so I just began to write down the most important lessons that I had learned in both positive and negative situations. These lessons revealed beliefs or convictions that had shaped me. Once I was at this point, I was able to write them out as values and I was able to see that there were categories. I realized that as I wrote them down that they were "my" values, not other people's.

Here are the categories that I wrote values for: personal relationship with God, personal leadership, worship, ministry of the Word, prayer, evangelism, training ministry, and building ministry structures. I have realized as I looked back at this document that it would be a great idea to go back through it and see what has stayed the same, what has changed, and what other categories have become important.

Let me give you a couple of examples and share with you how these values have affected me. Please remember that these are my values expressed in my own words to help me articulate what I believe. They are not written down as theological arguments or in order of importance, but as personal insights.

1. Personal relationship with God: *God is seeking relationship with us*. What I mean by this is that all relationship begins with God. He initiates it. He makes it possible. He does all the "hard work." This value lies at the foundation for the way that I speak about God. It lies at the foundation of all discipleship.

In ministry settings where I influence the atmosphere, I want to make sure that it is clear that God is pursuing us. God is the one who closes the gap between him and us. He is coming to us. This is a huge difference from thinking that somehow I have to get to God or get it right in order to find him.

2. Training ministry: *Leaders who train others need to take the word "failure" out of the training environment*. The only real failure is a person who is not learning or not trying. If we are trying and encouraged to continue trying, we will be learning. When this happens, we are not failing. This value does not require a great deal of explanation. You can imagine how this changes the training environment.

3. Ministry structure: *Organization and structure should follow life"*. I first learned this from John Wimber who used to teach us that, "organism (life) first, organization (structure) to follow." Or in other words, in the ministry setting find out what God is breathing life into and add the necessary structure that will help it sustain and flourish.

This makes a big difference in the way I evaluate structure and make decisions about what structures are needed.

These personal values have really helped me to think through each ministry settings. Having the list of personal values, I am able to evaluate ministry settings and look for resonance.

Effective Methodologies

Reviewing the lessons that we have learned and articulating ministry values will open the doors for identifying key methodologies and breakthrough concepts that move us towards effectiveness. The process of articulating a ministry philosophy will help us to identify the ministry methodologies that can be built on over a lifetime.

The identification of our values and methodologies that match our giftedness is a critical part of looking for the right ministry role. This is the topic of the next chapter.

Evaluation and Application:

1. What does an effective philosophy of ministry look like? And why is it important?

2. How does "giftedness" (spiritual gifts, natural abilities, and acquired skills) relate to an effective philosophy of ministry?

3. What is resonance and why is it important for owning your philosophy of ministry and functioning effectively from it?

4. What is the role of personal values in discovering and developing your philosophy of ministry? Why is an understanding of core values important for developing your philosophy of ministry?

5. What are your core values and your philosophy of ministry? Are you satisfied with your current understanding of this? If not, what action steps do you plan to take to gain clarity on these important issues?

Chapter 10

Finding the Right Role

At the beginning of 1996, I (Richard) came to one of those important moments in life. I was in the middle of a major decision-making process. My wife Lora and I believed that God was asking us to consider a major shift of direction. In order to understand the context of the decision, I will give you a few basic details.

I was 37 years old and had just finished my doctor of ministry (D.Min.) degree a couple of years earlier. My father and I had launched a leadership training ministry and I was beginning to teach more and more classes at Fuller Seminary and enjoying some success there. I really enjoyed co-ministry with my father both at Fuller and in other training contexts. In addition to this, I had planted a church that was beginning to take shape and had some real potential for growth and development. Lora and I were able to buy a townhouse and life seemed to be settling down. Our roots were sinking down, however, something else was also going on. I had a nagging sensation that God was up to something new and I could not dismiss the feeling.

The reason why I could not just dismiss this feeling was because of an experience during a prayer time in 1985. I had one of those powerful times when God spoke about his plan for my life. We call this a sense of destiny experience. In this experience, God spoke to me about a 10 year training process that he would lead me through. Between 1985-1995, what God had told me about had come to pass and as a result I was expecting that a new ministry role would emerge. I was looking for God's leading and listening for God's voice. The situation with the church plant in California, teaching at Fuller, and doing the leadership ministry with my father had all started before 1995. Was the situation that I was in the fulfillment? I wasn't sure.

Switzerland?

In 1995, while Lora and I were teaching some seminars in Switzerland, we both had an experience with God. We were consulting a group of leaders who wanted to see an evangelistic breakthrough in Zurich. They shared with me some disturbing statistics and trends about what was happening to the church in Switzerland. My advice was, "Plant new churches." They responded, "That is easy to say but not so easy to do." They agreed that Switzerland needed new churches, but their ministry was not involved in planting churches. They said, "We could help someone else do it. If someone else would lead the church plant, we would help." I said, "Well you better ask God to show you someone who could do that."

Later that day while hiking, I reflected on what they had shared. A little voice crept into my mind, "Richard, why don't you move to Switzerland and do it?" I looked at Lora and started to say something and thought "no way." I decided not to say anything about this to her. About six months later, Lora and I were chatting about ministry and the topic of Switzerland came up. We had to evaluate and decide if we would go back in 1996 to do more seminars. I casually shared my wild idea and it turned out that she had the exact same thought about moving to Switzerland while we had been hiking that day, but had also dismissed it quickly. My nagging sensation about something new was now changing into something that I needed to take very seriously. Could this be God?

To make a long story a little short, we believed that it was God and began to prayerful investigate moving toward relocating to Switzerland which we eventually did. Although we are no longer living there, we enjoyed nearly 12 years of ministry there before returning to the U.S. a couple of years ago. There were many things that God used to confirm the move to Switzerland. One of the most important things has to do with the subject of this chapter: focused living.

Four Factors of a Focused Life

During this same period of time, my father finished his book called *Strategic Concepts*. In this book, he identified four key factors that help leaders move into what he was calling a focused life. These factors are: 1. unique purpose, 2. unique role, 3. unique methodologies, and 4. ultimate contributions.

He wrote, "As a leader moves toward focus, the job description will usually have to be adapted so that these functions will line up with the leader's life purpose or effective methodologies. Such a role, which enhances focus is called the major role" (J. R. Clinton, p. 123).

I thought, "If this situation in Switzerland is God's direction for us, it will allow me to move into more focus than my current situation." I decided to try it out and see if the group in Switzerland would agree. I sent them a list of core values that made up my ministry philosophy. I wrote, "For me to lead the church it would have to be based on these core values." I included a summary of my destiny experiences and what I believed that God had called me to do. I told them that I would need some flexibility and financial support to do this. I outlined a job description that would uniquely fit what I believed my ministry role would be. It seemed really idealistic to me, but God confirmed it as the group in Switzerland invited us to come and lead them. By knowing something about focused living, I was able to take steps toward a ministry role that was shaped around my destiny, my ministry philosophy, and my giftedness that would allow me to become more focused.

What Makes Up Focus in Mid-Life?

When we move into the mid-life, there are three issues that are critical for our leadership development when we look at becoming focused. First, we need to operate out of a clear sense of God's calling and understanding of what God wants us to do. Second, we need to have a ministry role that allows our unique giftedness to be used and provides a ministry platform for us to do what God has called us to do. Third, we need to use methodologies that are consistent with the ministry philosophy that God has shaped into us. These three issues allow ministry to flow out of our being the person who God has made us to be.

One of the problems that many of us face as we navigate the challenges of mid-life is that we simply do not know ourselves very well and we have not clarified God's purposes for our lives. We have not identified our giftedness. In addition to this, many of us have not worked on understanding or articulating our ministry values and philosophy. Becoming a leader who is increasingly more focused and intentional on accomplishing God's purposes does not happen automatically. In fact, the opposite seems to be true. Most of us tend to drift along in life and leadership or we jump from one thing to the next. We become unfocused and scattered leaders. Working to articulate these three issues will help each one of us to move closer to God and closer to accomplishing God's purposes in our lives.

Finding the Right Role

As we come into the middle stages of our leadership development, we need a role or platform for leadership and ministry that allows us the freedom to effectively accomplish God's purposes for our lives. Unfortunately, ideal leadership and ministry roles are not waiting for most leaders. The reality is that we will have to adapt available roles to better fit who we are. Every role will contain a mix of elements, some that we want to focus our time and energy on and some that we do not. That is reality, but the goal is to minimize those things that we are not necessarily called to while maximizing those that we are called to. This allows us freedom to do what we were created for.

There are certain things that all of us have to do as leaders. For example, we need a job description that gives us guidelines for our ministry activity. We need to know what the boundaries are. We need to know what areas we have responsibility for and what areas we do not. We need a ministry role that gives us recognition, status, and credibility to do what God has called us to do. Along with a clear job description, leaders need adequate authority and resources in order to do an effective job. Things like the appropriate kind of support, equipment, and resources are critical for success.

Leaders also need appropriate freedom to adapt their jobs to use their uniqueness to full effectiveness. Our uniqueness is a blend of our gift mix; lessons learned from our life experiences, values picked up along the way, and the methodologies that we have learned.

Sometimes it is possible to adapt a ministry role and sometimes it is not. It normally takes about 10 to 15 years of ministry experience before a leader truly knows what kind of ministry role would best fit their uniqueness. There are various reasons for this. It takes time for ministry values to be shaped and recognized, it takes time for giftedness to emerge, and it takes a variety of ministry experiences to discover methodologies that work well for the individual leader.

Basic Guidelines for Finding the Right Role

Each leader is unique and God's timetable for each leader is unique. There are many factors that affect the pace of a leader's development. This makes it very difficult to predict exactly when the issue of finding the right kind of ministry role becomes important, but if you look at enough life stories of leader's you begin to observe some tendencies. There are some general tendencies that are helpful to share. Here are some basic guidelines that might help you identify where you are in the process.

The First 10 Years - In the first 10 years or so of ministry, the emphasis should be on gaining ministry experience. I encourage every leader to get as many different kinds of ministry experiences as they can. Different ministry experiences will help in identifying giftedness. Giftedness emerges over time and giftedness emerges based on the ministry needs of the situation. We have observed that leaders will tend to drift towards ministries and other leaders who are using giftedness similar to their own. Many people may not even be aware that they are drifting towards these ministry settings. They will just notice that there is an inner attraction and they will discover a longing to learn how to do what they see going on.

As a leader gets involved in serving in various ministry settings, they will learn how to use their giftedness effectively. It takes repeated efforts, some evaluation, and some reflection from others to help the leader move towards effectiveness. In addition to learning how to use their giftedness effectively, the leader will usually begin the process of clarifying ministry values and allowing a ministry philosophy to be formed in them. This takes time to emerge and usually involves some trial and error or on-the-job training.

My recommendation to younger emerging leaders, who are in the first ten years of ministry, is to try to take a variety of ministry roles. Start with the ones that you are excited about and start learning. Pay attention to the ministry roles and ministry settings where you "come alive" and feel at home, but do not limit yourself to just those things that you like or feel attracted to. Try other areas of ministry activity as well. Sometimes you might be surprised at what you learn about yourself and you might discover whole parts of your calling, destiny, or giftedness that you were not aware of.

The Second 10 Years - After about 10 years or so of ministry, the leader should be able to identify their most satisfying ministry roles and experiences as well as the least satisfying. With this in mind, whenever possible, begin to move towards ministry roles that fit your giftedness, values, and philosophy and allow you to keep learning how to become more effective. Often, a leader does not have the possibility to make this happen. In these situations, I recommend being faithful and patient where you are until the right opportunity presents itself. Knowing what you are looking for will make you more sensitive to the right opportunities when they come. Whenever it is possible, make little changes to the ministry role that you are currently serving in that help you move closer to a ministry role that fits you.

When you begin to feel constrained by the ministry role, it is usually time to start moving towards a better fit. There are signs that begin to point a leader in this direction of change. These may include feeling unsettled, increasing frustration, increasing interest in other ministry areas, etc. When trying to decide what is the best role a leader should try:

1. To move into ministry roles that provide a better match between the responsibilities of the ministry role and their giftedness. Speak to the other leaders involved in your situation, both leaders above you as well as leaders who are peers. Share what is happening and be open to the suggestions that they share with you. Ask God to replace things like frustration and unsettledness with vision. Ask God to give you his perspective on what is happening to you. You may be on the edge of a transition or issues could be surfacing that need some healing from God.

2. To create more freedom to choose ministry assignments. Sometimes we cannot choose, but when we can make choices, learn to say "Yes" to the ministry tasks that take you a step closer to focusing on God's purposes. Learning to say "No" to ministry assignments that are not moving you in the right direction is equally important.

3. To move into ministry contexts that better align with your values and allow you to use the methodologies that fit best.

The Third 10 Years - If you are not in a ministry role that fits you well after 20 years or so, you have to be more proactive. It could be that you do not really know yourself well enough. It could be that the ministry setting you are in is not flexible enough to adapt a role to fit you. If God has clearly called you to be in that ministry setting, then stay there and accept it. Serve God faithfully and recognize that focus for you is not about finding the right ministry role. It is about fulfilling God's purposes in that ministry setting. It might be that God's emphasis will be on living out values and using your ministry methodologies to model something important for that ministry setting.

For other leaders who have some flexibility to make changes, be proactive. Identify the kind of ministry role that would fit you best. Design an ideal ministry role, a dream role, and then ask the question, "How could I move towards this?" Wherever it is possible, you should try to adapt your ministry role to fit you as exactly as possible. It should be based on a clear understanding of God's purposes for your life, your clearly defined giftedness, and a ministry context that allows you to flow naturally in ministry according to your values and your philosophy. Rarely does a leader get everything they want from a ministry role. But any steps we can take to move towards focus are good.

The Forth 10 Years - At this point, we are talking about leaders who have been in ministry for 40 or more years. Not very many leaders make it to this stage. This can be a very special season of ministry. The emphasis shifts from finding the right ministry role to consolidating what God has done through your life. The emphasis of being a focused leader shifts to multiplying and investing what God has given you into others. This is the legacy that you will leave behind. Most importantly, the emphasis shifts to celebrating a lifetime of faithfully serving God.

The ministry role is no longer as important as it once was. A lifetime of faithful ministry has created opportunities to influence other people. Investing, empowering, and multiplying in others what God has done in you should be the emphasis. A leader in this stage will need a ministry role that gives them the opportunities to do these kinds of activities. More than likely a leader in this stage will be looking at transitioning out of direct influence in ministry settings to more indirect influence. They will be passing the baton on to the next generation of leaders.

Writing Out a Ministry Role Description

No matter where you are in your process of leadership development it can help to write down what you have learned so far. It is very helpful to write out a paragraph that describes a ministry role that uniquely fits you. What you write summarizes your understanding of what kind of role utilizes your giftedness and allows you to minister out of being. You can use what God has given you and you can operate out of a set of values and methodologies that you have learned along the way.

The paragraph can begin with, "In terms of my giftedness and my past experience in various roles, I know that I need a ministry role that allows me to ..." Then you may want to try to write down key phrases and words that describe the kind of role that allows you to flow in your giftedness and use the ministry insights or methodologies.

For example, here is what I wrote to the group in Switzerland. I wrote it in faith as though everything that God had revealed to me in visions about the future was going to happen. I wrote:

> "My role will need to be multi-faceted. In addition to leading the new church, I will operate out of this church as a trainer, teacher, and work with leaders. I will be involved in a teaching ministry in other churches, courses, workshops, seminars and conferences. I will also be involved in mentoring and in the training of mentors. I will especially focus building up training programs for younger upcoming leaders."

Along with this, I shared with them my five unique methodologies that strongly influence my ministry:

1. I am absolutely dependent on God for effectiveness in ministry. Jesus' model of only doing what he saw the Father doing and only speaking the words that his Father gave him is the primary model of dependence. In every conversation, meeting or ministry situation, I will week to discern what the Father is doing as he reveals that through the Holy Spirit and I will cooperate with what he is doing.

2. I will choose to be vulnerable and transparent in life and ministry and choose communication styles that reveal this. I will count on God's promise that he will take this and use it for his glory. I will intentionally model transparency.

3. I will seek to demonstrate a deep and thorough knowledge of the Scriptures in order to release God's truth in powerful ways and gain credibility in my ministry. This is based on the conviction that personal familiarity with the Bible conveys competence.

4. I will use J. Robert Clinton's leadership developmental frameworks to help leaders gain perspective on their lives and ministry with the goal of helping them live God-honoring lives.

5. I will actively seek to create effective training environments everywhere I go in order to see people strengthened, matured, and equipped for life and ministry.

When I sent this, I wondered how they would respond. They liked the clarity and it gave them something to work with. They wrote a job description based on it and incorporated these values and methodologies into the philosophy of the church.

My ministry role was shaped to fit the needs of the situation and it was shaped to fit what I shared with them. It was a great experience.

As I am writing this, I can look back over the experience in Switzerland. I can honestly say that it worked better than I imagined. The role fit me and allowed me to be me. It allowed me to operate in greater and greater effectiveness and was a wonderful and rewarding experience.

Writing a clear paragraph about your giftedness and identifying the kind of ministry role that best fits you will help you. When you have a chance to move towards a role that better fits who you are, prayerfully consider taking it and allowing God to further develop you. In making your choice, remember that there is no perfect role waiting out there. You will have to adapt a role to fit you and there are some aspects of every ministry role that might not be a part of your "ideal role."

Do not be in a hurry to try to find an ideal role. Leadership development is not a sprint. I have seen too many younger leaders (those in the first 10 years or so of ministry experience) change roles too quickly. Many want to only do things they like or things that they are good at and miss opportunities where God could have taught them important and necessary lessons.

My father gave some great advise when he wrote about finding an ideal role, "Without dreams of what we can be, few of us will ever get there" (*Strategic Concepts*, p. 153). So keep dreaming and allowing God to move you into the ministry roles that best fit who he has designed you to be.

The Main Issue: Focusing on the Main Thing

Remember at every stage of development you are not just choosing what you like or want to do. This is not the main issue. The main thing is God's purposes for your life. He is the Lord, the sovereign Creator, and the great Designer. As leaders, the main thing to focus on is following his plan in humble obedience.

Our focus needs to be on him. As I heard one preacher say, "The best place for a sheep to be is directly behind the Shepherd." That is what our understanding of leadership development is all about. It is not about what we want or what we think would be best for us. Sometimes God asks us to do things that we might not like but is a part of our leadership development that moves us towards our destiny. Through obedience to his will we can learn critical lessons that could not have been learned in any other way.

If God is moving you towards a more focused ministry role, there will be clear guidance from him. He will help you understand what is going on and help you make good decisions. These decisions, when they are led by God, will move you into roles that better match who you are, allow you to go forward in your development, and prepare you to finish well and leave a lasting legacy.

Evaluation and Application:

1. What are the four key factors that help produce a focused Life? Where are you at in your understanding of each of these?

2. What is meant by "ideal ministry (or leadership) role"? How does a leader go about finding or creating this ideal role?

3. How do ministry philosophy, ideal role, and unique methodologies work together in a focused life?

4. Why is focus so important in mid-life? How are you doing? What might you do to gain a better, more clear sense of life focus?

5. What is your ideal role? What are you doing or can you do to work toward realizing your unique role?

Chapter 11

Accountability and Mentoring

In the late 80s, I (Paul) was an Associate Pastor at a large church in Southern California. My first year on staff had been exciting and had gone pretty well, but now in my second year things were beginning to get a little crazy. I was discovering that church ministry was very different from the public arena, that working with volunteers was very different from working with paid staff, and that there was a certain aspect of "spiritual warfare" that I had not encountered in the past. All of this led me to a time of struggle and self-doubt that seemed to get more difficult with the passing days.

One day, Richard Clinton, an Assistant Pastor on our staff who worked with young adults, stopped by my office for a chat. We were friends who both had a sense of calling to work with younger emerging leaders. Richard was also going through his own challenges so we would talk, listen, and pray together. On that day though, Richard asked me if I would like to go to breakfast with him and his father later in the week.

Richard's father was J. Robert (Bobby) Clinton, who taught leadership courses at Fuller Seminary. He had recently written a book entitled *The Making of a Leader* that I had read and found helpful. I was excited about this opportunity and eagerly accepted Richard's invitation.

The Napkin That "Read My Mail"

At the breakfast later that week, we chatted for a while and then Bobby asked me to tell him about myself - family background, conversion experience, career path, marriage and family experience, and current ministry. As I shared he would occasionally jot something on a paper napkin while listening or asking another open-ended question. After about a half an hour he seemed satisfied with what he had heard and asked me if he could share some insights with me.

He took the napkin in hand and began to read my mail. He gave me a perspective on my life and current challenges that shook me to the core while giving me a sense of God's sovereign leading and work in my life. As he shared, he would give me opportunities to ask clarifying questions and then respond in ways that gave me clarity and hope.

At the end of our breakfast meeting, Bobby said that he would me willing to meet with me again, but first I would need to read through his *Leadership Emergence Theory* manual (434 pages). He said, "Once you have read through and understand the leadership emergence concept, give me a call and we can set up a time to meet."

To be honest, this assignment was a little (or a lot) overwhelming. Bobby's manual was very detailed and written in "Clintonese." It was difficult going at first, but his insight from the Bible about how God develops a leader over a lifetime was profound and transformational. As I read on, I began to get it and found myself reading late into the night for a week or so until I had finished the entire manual. As I read through the manual I began to understand at least the basic concepts and generated a list of questions.

When I called Bobby a week or so after our first meeting he was surprised. He asked me if I had read the manual and understood the concept. I told him that I had read it, that I thought I understood the basic concepts, and that I had several questions that I would like to ask him. We set a date for a follow up breakfast to discuss my reading and questions. We met about once a month for the next six months until I transitioned from the ministry position I was in and moved to Northern California.

Little did I know at the time that Bobby would become a primary influence in my life and leadership. We all need mentors in our lives. We need others who believe in us, take us seriously, and are willing to invest in our lives. Bobby (and several others) has been this for me and I am eternally grateful.

Mentors are especially important at three strategic points in a leader's life and development: when they are first starting out, when they are navigating mid-life, and when they must make strategic choices for focused living so that they can finish well. In this chapter we will focus on mentoring for navigating mid-life challenges and opportunities.

Help! I Need a Mentor

Over the last several years, I have had the opportunity to write, teach classes, conduct seminars, and lead workshops on mentoring. One of the things that I have discovered while doing these is that very few leaders have been intentionally mentored and that most leaders are desperate for mentoring. Everywhere I go I hear the cry, "Help! I need a mentor."

Mentoring has become a popular buzzword in the business, education, and ministry realms. There are literally dozens of books being published on mentoring and coaching (the new buzz word). Leaders are familiar with the concept but (in my opinion) very few are being effectively mentored or effectively mentoring others.

As I mentioned in chapters 4-6, mentoring is critical for accountability and development in mid-life. Specifically, there are several reason why we need mentoring. These reasons include:

- … because we live in a relational dysfunctional age.
- … because our individualism is causing burdens too heavy to hold up under.
- … because we need others to mature as whole people.
- … because we can save ourselves a lot of grief if we can establish healthy
- accountability with others.
- … because we have something to offer others.

What is Mentoring?

Clinton defines mentoring as "a relational experience in which one person *empowers* another by sharing God-given resources" (*Connecting*, p. 33, italics added). I have a couple of definitions of my own that maybe helpful:

- Transformational relationships.
- Friendships with Godly purpose and outcome.

Whatever definition works for you, the bottom line is that mentoring involves relational empowering or doing life together. Clinton goes on to describe a continuum that identifies several types of mentoring relationships with different levels of involvement and types of empowering:

Intensive Mentoring (intentional, regular, short-term)

- Discipler – establishing basics of following Christ
- Spiritual Guide – establishing spiritual disciplines
- Coach – motivation and skill development

Occasional Mentoring (circumstantial, regular/irregular, short-term/ongoing)

- Counselor – perspective and advise for relationships and life circumstances
- Teacher – knowledge and understanding of specific topic
- Sponsor – career guidance, protection, and promotion

Passive Mentoring (inadvertent, vicarious)

- Divine Contact – person, word, and/or circumstances used to confirm God's will
- Contemporary Model – living model for life and ministry
- Historical Model – deceased model of life and ministry

Note that each type of mentoring has different intensities of relationship and different outcomes related to empowering. Not every person is effective in all types of mentoring. We need to know our needs in order to effectively enter into healthy mentoree relationships and we need to know our spiritual gifts, abilities, and acquired skills (gift mix) along with our sense of calling to be able to best establish healthy mentoring relationships.

Is There a Spiritual Component to Mentoring?

Although some types of mentoring focus on skill or career development, spiritual development and transformation is inherent in all types of healthy Christian mentoring. Keith Anderson and Randy Reese, in *Spiritual Mentoring*, are especially helpful in clarifying this. They have expanded Clinton's mentoring paradigm to include the spiritual dynamics of empowering. They state that, "Spiritual mentoring is a triadic relationship between mentor, mentoree, and the Holy Spirit, where the mentoree can discover, through the already present action of God,

* Intimacy with God,
* Ultimate identity as a child of God, and
* A unique voice for kingdom responsibility." (p. 12)

For Anderson and Reese, mentoring involves the active work of the Holy Spirit in and through the relational interaction between mentor and mentoree that produces transformation in both parties.

Healthy Christian mentoring must not ignore this reality. As a mentoree or mentor we will be affected by the reality that we "reproduce in kind." We need to make sure that we are open to the work of the Holy Spirit in our lives, relationships, and ministries if we want to be empowered and give empowering to others.

What Are the Characteristics of Effective Mentors?

Effective mentors seem to have some common characteristics. Although, the only perfect mentor is God, effective mentors seem to have several (but probably not all) of the following characteristics. Mentors are in process along with their mentorees so effective mentoring tends to involve growth for both parties. The effective mentor (*Connecting*, p. 38) tends to have the:

- Ability to see potential in others.
- Tolerance of mistakes, brashness, abrasiveness, etc. in order to see potential developed.
- Flexibility in responding to people and circumstances.
- Patience, knowing that time and experience are needed for a person to develop potential.
- Perspective, having vision and ability to see down the road.
- Gifts and abilities to build up and encourage people.

These characteristics are both gift oriented and compassion oriented. A person's gift mix may aid in specific types of mentoring, but love is critical (I Corinthians 13: 1-3) for effective transformation and empowering. Even for the accomplished mentor, the relationship will be dynamic and transforming for all involved as each person learns to love God and one another.

How Do I Establish Healthy Mentoring Relationships?

Establishing a healthy mentoring relationship can be pretty intimidating, especially at first. We may have need and desire for mentoring, but what if no one initiates a relationship or we initiate and the person turns us down? Mentoring can lead to difficult relational issues that can cut to the core of who we are, our insecurities, and our tolerance for ambiguity.

Over the years, I have learned a few things about establishing healthy mentoring relationships. I have been pretty fortunate in that several leaders have initiated relationships with me over the years. I have learned that this is pretty unusual and that few folks have this kind of experience. Even so, there have been times when I have been without mentoring or have had a need for specific types of mentoring.

One of the first things that I learned was that mentoring relationships were a priority to me. I needed them and valued them. If a mentor did not initiate, then I needed to prayerfully initiate.

Secondly, I have learned that mentors are not God; they are human (and so am I). This means that I need to be careful about the expectations that I have for mentoring and that I need to recognize that mentoring at best is a pretty human encounter (with the resources of God available). With this in mind, here are some steps that I would suggest that you consider in initiating mentoring relationships:

1. Prayerfully identify your need and type of mentoring.

2. Prayerfully identify potential mentors.

3. Initiate a first meeting (I usually ask the person out for coffee, breakfast, or lunch as my guest).

4. Begin developing the relationship with the perspective mentor by sharing your desire for mentoring.

5. If the person is open to mentoring you, define the parameters of the relationship (goals, type of mentoring, expectations, time frame, etc.).

6. Follow through on all appointments, assignments, and commitments.

7. Incorporate periodic times of feedback and evaluation into the relationship to assess how the mentoring relationship is going.

8. Develop a transition strategy for when the formal mentoring relationship is completed.

There are several dynamics that interact together in mentoring relationships that can be helpful to understand. They include: (1) attraction and responsiveness; (2) setting healthy boundaries; and (3) accountability and empowering.

1. **Attraction and responsiveness:** Attraction is critical for the first stage of the mentoring relationship and is usually mutual. The mentoree is attracted to the mentor because of something that the mentoree values or desires to have in their life or ministry. The mentor sees potential in the mentoree and wants to help develop it. The mentoree and the mentor may have similar gifts or callings. There is a chemistry that attracts them to each other.

The experienced mentor will test the faithfulness of the mentoree before making a commitment to mentoring. Attraction is not enough to empower, the issue of responsiveness must be addressed. Is the mentoree teachable? Is he willing to be accountable for character or ministry growth? Will the mentoree show up on time for scheduled appointments? Will he complete assignments to the best of his ability? These issues must be resolved in a responsible fashion if the mentoring relationship is to be effective for transformation and empowering.

2. **Setting healthy boundaries:** Many of us look to others for strength or wisdom, especially in times of uncertainty or crisis. This is not necessarily wrong or bad, but can turn into "co-dependency" if we do not establish healthy boundaries for our mentoring relationships.

Unmet expectations are one of the major reasons why mentoring relationships do not work out. Mentorees can tend to expect too much from their mentors. They need to remember that mentoring is not marriage or adoption. Healthy mentoring is an adult relationship in which empowering takes place so that all parties grow in their dependence on God and their ability to trust him in a variety of situations - good, bad, and ugly.

Setting healthy boundaries is essential for framing realistic expectations in a mentoring relationship. Realistic expectations can help limit potential drama and hurt in a relationship. Healthy boundaries should include discussion and agreement on such issues as: type of mentoring, scheduled meetings, homework assignments, time frame for formal mentoring relationship, when it is appropriate to call, and transitioning.

Addressing issues of confidentiality and trust are critical at this juncture of the relationship. Healthy relationships are based on trust. Careless sharing of information discussed in a mentoring context that gets back to one of the folks involved in the mentoring relationship can be devastating. Boundaries for confidentiality must be established and consistently implemented!

Even if you establish realistic and healthy boundaries, there will be issues that arise as you get to know each other. Over time our humanity tends to surface and we will have to deal with the stuff of life in gracious and redemptive ways. This is where the dynamics of the relationship can lead to transformation and growth.

3. **Accountability and empowering:** Clinton describes four ranges of accountability and empowering in mentoring relationships. His constellation model includes upward, downward, and peer (internal and external) mentoring. The following diagram illustrates these four ranges:

Diagram 6: Constellation Model

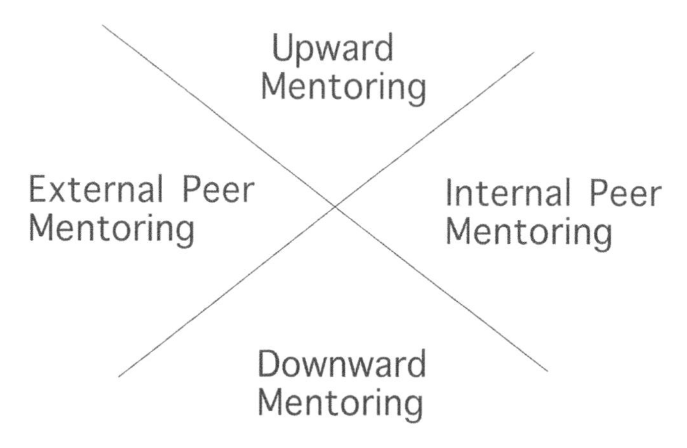

Upward and downward mentoring involve a relationship between a more mature, experienced person and a less mature, experienced one. We all need upward mentoring to help us with needs that we have, but we also need to be involved in downward mentoring where we help younger emerging leaders with their growth and development.

Peer mentoring is between people who have similar levels of maturity and experience. Internal peer mentoring is between people who have common organizational or social contexts. External peer mentoring is between people who do not share common organizational or social contexts.

Mentors can become trusted friends and colleagues who we can be honest with, who can hold us accountable, or who can support us when we are struggling. Ideally, we need to be involved in all four of these kinds of mentoring relationships. But in a less than perfect world, we will probably have to be pretty intentional and at times creative if we are to have all or even some of these kinds of accountable and empowering relationships.

Remember, that when we are not involved in or cannot find suitable mentoring relationships, we can be involved in passive mentoring (contemporary and historical models). It is helpful to learn from others who are ministering effectively or who have ministered effectively in the past. Popular books, biographies, and DVDs can all be sources for empowering while we are in between person-to-person mentoring relationships.

Empowering for Transformation

Mentoring can be a powerful means of being empowered and empowering others. I like to think of spiritual mentoring as a relationally based process of empowerment that results in both parties growing spiritually. Spiritual mentoring is mutual and based in a Biblical understanding of relationships that are "mutually submitted to Christ and one another" (Ephesians 5: 21). What do I mean by empowerment? I define it in the following way:

Empowerment involves transformational relationships in which all participants come to a healthier understanding and experience of their God-given potential as individuals, members of social networks, and members of a community who serve and empower others.

Let's look at each aspect of empowerment a little closer:

1. *Transformational Relationships* involve caring and sharing of life experiences and resources.

2. *Mutually Empowering* involves the healthy growth of all parties involved.

3. *Understanding and Experiencing God-Given Potential* involves the transformational work of the Word of God and the Holy Spirit to change us so that we become more like Christ in character, perspective, and behavior while discovering our uniqueness as God's "human" creation.

4. *Serve and Empower Others* involves the understanding that realizing our unique potential in God connects us to others in empowering ways through service.

According to J. Robert Clinton (*Connecting*, p. 95-96) there are eight major empowerment functions possible in healthy spiritual mentoring relationships:

1. Encouragement
2. Soundboard
3. Evaluation
4. Perspective
5. Advise
6. Networking
7. Guidance
8. Healing

How Did Jesus Effectively Mentor Others?

In II Timothy 2: 2, Paul exhorts his younger protégé Timothy to "entrust to reliable men [the things you have heard me say in the presence of many witnesses]... who will also be qualified to teach others." (NIV) Paul was reminding Timothy of what Barnabas had done for him (and what Baranabas had probably learned from watching Jesus).

Robert Coleman, in *The Master Plan of Evangelism*, suggests that Jesus had a strategic and systematic approach to develop disciples who would become the primary leaders in establishing and the rapid expansion of the Church as a community of believers committed to taking the Gospel to the ends of the earth. Based on the earlier research of A.B. Bruce, *The Training of the Twelve*, Coleman described the following characteristics of Jesus' strategy:

1. Selection
2. Association
3. Consecration
4. Impartation
5. Demonstration
6. Delegation
7. Supervision
8. Reproduction

An examination of Jesus' disciple-making strategy in the Gospels reveals that:

- Jesus proclaimed the "gospel of repentance" (Matthew 4: 17).

- Jesus ministered to the crowds (Matthew 4:25) but also called a few to "follow" him and become his personal disciples (Matthew 4: 19).

- Jesus' strategy for public ministry was to travel from town to town teaching, preaching, and ministering to needy people (Matthew 4: 23-24).

- While he was doing this he invested personally in a few who had responded to his call ((Matthew 5: 1-2).

His disciple-making strategy involved the following stages:

1. Teaching about true discipleship (Matthew 5-7).

2. Showing them how to minister in the power of the Holy Spirit (Matthew 8: 1-9: 34).

3. Sharing with them the burden of God for the lost (Matthew 9: 35-38).

4. Sending them out two-by-two to practice what they had heard and seen (Matthew 10).

5. Debriefing them (Luke 10 – after sending out of the 72).

6. Co-ministering with them (Matthew 11-23).

7. Preparing them to minister on their own (Matthew 16: 21-28; Matthew 20: 17-19).

8. Commissioning them to make disciples (Matthew 28: 18-20).

I agree with Coleman (and Bruce) that Jesus was intentional in his disciple-making strategy and that his strategy is to be a primary strategy for the church throughout history and across cultures. It is not the only way to make disciples, but a primary way. Theological training via Bible colleges, seminaries, distance learning, seminars, and conferences can be helpful, but they are never a replacement for the empowering that can take place in a face-to-face relationship.

Key to implementing the Jesus model for disciple-making and leadership development is selection. Future leaders emerge out of discipleship pools.

Selection

Richard Clinton (*Selecting and Developing Emerging Leaders*) suggests the following characteristics for assessing a potential leader for mentoring and leadership development. These characteristics include:

- Appetite for the Word of God.
- Orientation toward application of the Word of God.
- Orientation toward holiness and righteousness.
- Orientation toward prayer (and other spiritual disciplines).
- Orientation towards hearing from God.
- Self-starting orientation.

Other characteristics that I look for include: faithfulness and an ability to follow through, being teachable and a willingness to be accountable, servant orientation and a willingness to do the dirty work, and a passion for the Great Commission.

I have learned to test prospective mentorees in the area of faithfulness and follow through before initiating a formal mentoring relationship. Experience has taught me that if they are not faithful in little, they tend not to follow through when given greater responsibilities or faith opportunities.

One of the most powerful examples of a person who implemented the Jesus model in the New Testament was Barnabas. Let's take a look at his life and see what we can learn:

Barnabas, Paul (and Timothy and...) and John Mark

Text: "Joseph, a Levite from Cyprus, whom the apostles called Barnabas (which means Son of Encouragement) sold a field he owned and brought the money and put it at the apostle's feet." (Acts 4: 36-37, NIV)

Overview of Barnabas' life:

- He was a good man, full of the Spirit, who was an effective evangelist (Acts 11: 24)

- He befriended Paul in Jerusalem (while others were afraid that Paul was using the guise of conversion to infiltrate the inner circle of Church leaders) and introduced him to the apostles after his conversion on the road to Damascus (Acts 9: 27)

- He was sent by the apostles in Jerusalem to Antioch to check out the Gentile revival there (Acts 11: 22)

- He traveled to Tarsus to find Paul (many years after Paul's conversion, see Galatians 1: 13 – 2: 1) and take him to Antioch where they co-minister as prophets and teachers (Acts 13: 1) for one year (Acts 11: 26)

- During a worship service (while they were fasting) Barnabas and Paul were prophetically "set apart" for evangelism and church planting in Asia Minor (Acts 13: 2)

- After a time of fasting and prayer, the leaders laid hands on them to commission them and send them off (Acts 13: 3)

- They took John Mark along with them and planted several churches in Cyprus and Asia Minor (Acts 13-14)

- While in Pamphylia, John Mark "deserted" Barnabas and Paul (Acts 15: 37)

- During this church planting trip the leadership of the team changed from Barnabas to Paul (Acts 13: 13)

- Upon their return to Antioch they reported what God had done through them to the church (Acts 14: 27) and they stayed there for awhile (Acts 14: 28)

- Paul and Barnabas attended the Council at Jerusalem to discuss the Gentile "issue" (Acts 15)

- Upon their return to Antioch, they (along with Judas and Silas) reported the results of the Council to the church (Acts 15: 30)

- Soon after their return to Antioch, Barnabas and Paul were led to revisit the churches they had planted in Asia Minor (Acts 15: 35-36)

- Barnabas wanted to take John Mark along, but Paul refused (because he had deserted them on the first trip). They had a "sharp" disagreement and decided to go their separate ways (Acts 15: 37-41, Barnabas took John Mark and sailed for Cyprus; and Paul chose Silas and traveled to Syria and Cilicia)

- While in Lystra, Paul recruited Timothy to be part of his team (Acts 16: 1-4)

- After their "split," Barnabas is not mentioned again directly in the Acts of the Apostles

The Rest of the Story:

- Much later, toward the end of Paul's life, he sent for John Mark because he had now proven himself to be "helpful to me in my ministry" (II Timothy 4: 11)

- Barnabas took a chance on both Paul and John Mark and over the long haul they both became effective leaders in the early church

- Paul learned from Barnabas about the importance of mentoring young emerging leaders (see I/II Timothy and Titus)

The Ten Commandments of Mentoring

J. Robert Clinton (*Connecting*) has developed The Ten Commandments of Mentoring that help give us an overview of what healthy mentoring looks like. These commandments are:

Commandment 1: Relationship – establish the mentoring relationship.

Commandment 2: Purpose – jointly agree upon the purpose of the mentoring relationship.

Commandment 3: Regularity – determine the regularity of interactions.

Commandment 4: Accountability – determine the type of accountability.

Commandment 5: Communication – set up communication mechanisms.

Commandment 6: Confidentiality – clarify the level of confidentiality.

Commandment 7: Life Cycle – establish the time frame for the mentoring relationship.

Commandment 8: Evaluation – periodically evaluate the relationship.

Commandment 9: Expectations – modify expectations to reflect real-life circumstances.

Commandment 10: Closure – bring timely closure to formal mentoring relationship.

We all need mentors and to be mentors for others. This application of "bearing one another's burdens" (Galatians 6: 2) is a partial fulfillment of the Great Commandment to love God and love our neighbor. It is also a sign or mark that we are becoming Christ-like and demonstrating the fruit of the Spirit.

The application of accountability and mentoring in mid-life is critical for finishing well. Without accountability we are vulnerable to burnout, blowout, and plateauing. Without developing a mentoring orientation we will probably miss one of the most important aspects of leaving a lasting legacy – that of investing in and empowering the next generation of leaders.

Evaluation and Application

1. Why do we need mentoring? Why do you need mentoring?

2. Who is mentoring you? Who are you mentoring?

3. How are you doing in your mentoring? What are you learning about mentoring? What are your strengths as a mentor? What are your weaknesses as a mentor? How can you use your strengths while becoming more effective in your areas of weakness?

4. What did you learn about mentoring and empowering from the example of Barnabas? How do you plan to apply this to your life and leadership?

5. Do you need a mentor? If so, what kind of mentoring do you need? How do you plan to go about finding the right mentor?

Chapter 12

Living and Leading Well

I (Richard) have met a lot of leaders who are excited about beginning things. They just love the start. They are energized and motivated during the build up to a launch point and are focused and their enthusiasm is contagious. I have also met some leaders who are closers. When they see the finish line, they hit another gear and release a burst of energy and power. They surge right to the end and close the deal. I cannot recall meeting very many leaders who love the middle part. I do not remember meeting many who live for the middle. The middle part is made up of the time when our start up energy is waning, the finish line is far away, and all the problems, barriers, and challenges start to pop up.

Recently, I was doing some pre-marital counseling sessions and I was struck by the passion, the love, the enthusiasm of the couple as they spoke about the beginning of their marriage relationship. I loved being with them and listening to them and watching them. It was so refreshing. My wife and I did the counseling sessions together and on our drives home, we reflected on our own marriage relationship and the contrast between where they were at the beginning and where we saw ourselves in the middle.

I will not share the details of our reflections except to say that the sessions caused us to remembered the energy and enthusiasm of our beginning. We also remembered many of the stretching and growing points we faced as challenges emerged in the last few decades. We sure would love to have some of that energy that we had when we started, but at the same time, we would not want to have to go through some of those challenging times again. We are glad some of those challenges are behind us. We learned so much. We grew and the foundations of our relationship were strengthened. The cracks in the foundations were exposed and we had to work on those issues. We know that what we have learned and experienced together will be what enables us to face what is yet to come.

In this book, we have been describing the mid-life or the two middle phases (ministry and leadership maturing and life maturing) of a leader's development. We have described many of the challenges and pointed out some of the traps to avoid. We have shared many insights and perspectives in order to help you navigate these times in your life. In this final chapter, I would like to share with you some reflections about a few Biblical leaders:

* King Saul
* Zechariah
* The Religious Leaders and Jesus
* Abram
* Martha
* Nicodemus
* Jeremiah

Before we take a look at these leaders, let me describe some major issues that are critical for our navigation of the challenges of mid-life ministry. As I thought and prayed about how to write this last chapter, I found myself reflecting on some of the key things that God has used to help me navigate the middle part of my leadership development journey. My prayer is that God will use these reflections to help you in your own journey through mid-life as you prepare to finish well (convergence) and establish a lasting legacy (afterglow).

Renewal in Mid-Life

Our leadership studies have revealed that leaders who do well over the middle phases of their leadership development are leaders who experience God's renewing touch on a regular basis. Over the years I have listened to leaders describe what happened to them when God brought a touch of his renewal into their lives. Listen to some of the words and phrases that leaders have used to describe their renewal experiences: refreshment, new strength, courage, growing faith, patience, fresh inspiration, renewed motivation, fresh desire, new energy, breakthrough concepts, and a re-focused life.

When I read a list like this, I find myself thinking, "Who wouldn't want to sign up to experience these things? Where can I sign up?" These are the kind of things that help a leader navigate mid-life challenges. Sometimes a leader is aware that they have reached a critical moment in their journey and they recognize the need for a touch from God. When we reach those moments, we tend to really cry out for God to intervene. Sometimes we are not aware of our need, but God is aware and intervenes with a touch of renewal. The central question is, "Are we open to God and willing to grow?" Openness to God is what gives God access to us and what gives us the opportunity to experience his renewing touch.

Openness

Openness is all about our attitude towards God and life. Most of us would like to think that we are very open people and would say, " I am open to God!" I cannot imagine any spiritual leader who would say that they are closed to God. All of us like to think that we are always open to God, but, if I am really honest, I wonder, "How open am I, really?

Paul wrote in I Corinthians 10 that the stories about what happened between God and his people were written down as examples for us (verse 6) to learn from. Paul described the people of the Exodus and how "God was not pleased with them" (verse 5). They had the pillar of cloud by day and the pillar of fire at night. They all walked with God through the desert. But they put God to the test (verse 9) because they "set their hearts on evil things" (verse 6). What happened to them demonstrates in a very graphic way that not all of them were open and willing to really follow God.

If we are honest, we have to ask ourselves some difficult questions about our own heart condition, "How open do you consider yourself to be?" "Are you open to God intervening in your life or do you want God to ask for your permission first?" "What if God uses some means that is outside of your experience or is God 'limited' to only certain acceptable methodologies?" "What if God uses a person that you would not expect him to use?" "Are you open to God using anyone to speak to you?" "Are you flexible enough to recognize God when he appears in ways that you are not used to?" "Are you flexible enough to receive what God wants to give you when he appears?" "Have you determined what God is allowed to do and what he is not allowed to do?" "Have you boxed God out of your paradigm?"

Open or Closed?

In John 1, John writes a prologue that introduced his telling a story about Jesus. He described Jesus as the Living Word who came to earth and how once he came to his own people they did not receive him and rejected him.

The word he uses which is translated "to receive" is a word used when a person speaks about hospitality. It is a relational term that describes how a guest should be treated and describes the extent to which you extend hospitality to your guest. In Middle Eastern cultures, hospitality is a huge deal. To receive someone into your home means you accept them, welcome them in, and allow them to make your home their home. In North America today, we often say, "make yourself at home." We may say this, but do we literally mean it?

Are we really that open to Jesus? In my own experience of following Jesus, I have gone through several stages of receiving him. First, I welcomed him in as my Savior. My relationship and openness to him was limited to my experiencing him in a saving role. Later on, I realized that there was something much deeper going on and I felt challenged to make what was described to me as "lordship surrender." Jesus was no longer just my Savior, now he became my lord and master. To receive Jesus is to welcome him into our whole life by asking him to take control of everything.

If we use the concept of hospitality and think of Jesus as a guest, "How have we received him?" Honestly, when I first asked Jesus to come into my life, I thought of him as being a guest, but he did not act like one. As it turned out, he was not someone who was just visiting and would soon leave. No, Jesus acted differently. He acted as though he wanted to move in and started to rearrange the furniture. He moved things around and changed all the routines and patterns of my life. He started to act as though he thought he owned the place! He became more than a casual guest and began to take up residence and ownership of everything.

Did this happen to you? How did you respond? Did you resist him and close off some areas of your life? It seems as though we all try to maintain some areas of control over our life. We try to get Jesus to back off and accept a consultant role or be a silent partner in our life venture. I do not think I consciously consult Jesus only when I need his help, but I do struggle with letting him have control of everything. Do you struggle with this as well? Let's be honest, we all know the struggle of surrendering control.

It is our attitude towards surrendering everything that determines whether we are open or closed to God's intervention in our lives. Our history with God and how we have experienced his renewing touch directly reflects on our level of openness. Leaders who are more open receive more from God. There are a number of reasons why we struggle to be open and there are a number of reasons why we are tempted to be closed. I want to make a few observations from some Biblical stories about people interacting with God. These stories are recorded to help us learn, grow, and ask ourselves questions about the process we are in with God.

King Saul

In 1 Samuel 15, we are told the story of what happened to cause God to reject King Saul. You probably know the details of the story, so I will jump right into some lessons that we can learn. I discovered two things that blocked King Saul and made him closed to what God wanted to do in and through him. First of all, there was his lack of full obedience. He was only partially obedient. Secondly, his impatience led him to try to find a shortcut to force God to do what he wanted.

I have had to face these issues in my own life from time-to-time. When we are only partially obedient we close off God by trying to take God's place. Think back on your own experience. Have you ever experienced the difference between partial obedience and full obedience? Maybe sometimes it was the difference between hedging your bets or being "all in." Have you sensitized yourself towards God enough to recognize the difference?

I often think about the situation Daniel's friends, Shadrach, Meshach, and Abednego, faced (Daniel 3). They were standing before an irate emperor and a fiery furnace. They demonstrated what it meant to be all in. They refused to bow and worship the emperor. They recognized the danger of telling him that; "You can throw us in the fire. Our God can rescue us..." and here is the part that really stands out to me, "but even if he doesn't, our faith is in him" (paraphrase of verses 16-18). That is being all in!

For me partial obedience feels a lot like conditional obedience. We try to negotiate with God so God will do what we ask... know what I mean? I have found myself at times partially obeying, but not fully obeying. For example, God gives me a word of knowledge in some public setting for a person that I do not know. He asks me to pray for the person. I say, "Okay, God" and then pray for them silently. I rationalize that God did not say "out loud" so I was obedient. Right? We have to watch out for this kind of thing. Partial obedience will close us off to God.

The second lesson I learned from studying King Saul is that impatience will close us off to God faster than anything else. Why? The answer is that impatience leads us to take things into our own hands. We try to assume God's place and make things happen. Where and how is God involved when we take over and try to do his part? Most of the time, he is not involved. We have cut him out. In the mid-life there are so many issues that cause us to lose our patience and try to take over. The example of King Saul should serve as a serious warning to us.

How are you doing in these two areas? Some of us might have closed ourselves to God and are not even aware of it. Are we willing to go all in? Are we willing to wait for God? My goal is to get better and better at the timing of God. I do not want to go faster than God through my impatience and I do not want to lag behind him through disobedience. I want to walk in step with God.

Zechariah

In Luke 1, we are told the story of what happened to Zechariah when God's messenger angel showed up. Zechariah was a God honoring man who was doing his normal priestly duties. He was doing exactly what he was supposed to be doing. He followed the pattern he had been taught and maintained the traditions of the priestly duties. His story is a warning to all of us who love routines, patterns, and traditions.

We have to be ready when God interrupts them! And we have to be ready for God to do something unexpected. The problem with routines, patterns, and traditions is that they can lead us to a place where we have a lack of expectation. It is a kind of spiritual dullness or spiritual lethargy.

That day at the temple was one of the greatest days in Zechariah's life. There are only a few people in the history that can tell a story about God intervening so dramatically in their lives. Even so, Zechariah was not ready to respond to God on that day. He did not respond in mature faith. Given his circumstances, I cannot really blame him. Can you?

I have been going to church and leading worship services for nearly thirty years. I do not tend to show up on a Sunday morning full of expectation that God will show up in some dramatic way and do something unexpected. I am very sympathetic to Zechariah. I imagine that I would have probably responded the same way. And because Zechariah was not ready to respond in faith, God silenced him until the promised son, John, was born. Can you imagine not being able to talk about the greatest thing that had ever happened to you? I cannot. After God opened his mouth, I imagine that Zechariah talked non-stop, at least for a short time.

Zechariah's story really challenges me because I really like routine. I like it when things function the way I expect them to or the way I have planned them to be. Do I really expect God to show up during my ministry routine? Would I allow him to interrupt me? Would I respond in faith to the unexpected, the unusual, or different ways that he might choose to move? How open am I?

The Religious Leaders and Jesus

When you read the gospel of John and you see the "unnamed" religious leaders mentioned, what do you think of them? In John 6-8, we are told stories about ongoing dialogues, arguments, debates, and interactions between Jesus and the religious leaders. Most of the time, I think of these religious leaders in negative ways.

Before going any further, let me say something positive about these religious leaders. They were the defenders of Israel's God and the defenders of Israel's faith. They saw their role as that of evaluating what was happening, making decisions about what was good, and rejecting what was wrong.

How many of us can identify with these religious leaders? I know I can. I cannot remember how many times I have been asked questions about this teaching or that doctrine, this leader or that phenomenon. "Richard, did you hear about what happened in that town or that place?" "What do you think? Is it God?" I get asked because people look to me as one of their spiritual leaders. They want me to help them evaluate what is happening. They want me to tell them if it is God or if it is right or wrong. The religious leaders around Jesus were just doing their job. The real problem was that they just were not doing their job very well.

When God showed up in an unexpected way, as a carpenter from Galilee, they did not recognize God. They listened to Jesus, watched what he did, and came to the conclusion that he was not a messenger of God. They concluded that Jesus was not a teacher sent from God, and for sure, he was not the Messiah or the Son of God as he claimed to be.

I often wonder how I would have reacted to Jesus if I were standing there listening to and watching him. I like to think that I would have been open enough to see God and I would have believed in him, but, I must confess, every time I have been confronted in my spiritual journey with something that was different from my experience or was outside of my expectations, I responded with a healthy skepticism. Every time I was confronted by something that was outside of the paradigms that I held, I responded with skepticism.

The first time I was in a place where the "power of God"' was healing people, I drew back. The first time I heard someone claim that God had spoken to him or her, I drew back. I had many good rational reasons why I found it hard to accept that it could be God. Experiences like these makes me wonder how I would have reacted if I had been around Jesus. Would I have missed God? I wonder how many times I have missed his presence because he showed up in a way that I did not expect him to or he showed up in a way that made me feel uncomfortable.

The religious leaders around Jesus developed a critical spirit and challenged him to prove himself. I believe that many of us miss God and his presence because we react to anything new or unusual with a critical and closed mindset. Please do not misunderstand; I am not saying we need to accept everything and everyone. Certainly, we need to be careful and evaluate. Paul said to, "test and evaluate" everything (I Thessalonians 5), but there is a big difference in the way we approach testing things if we have a critical spirit. Do you know what I mean? We can carefully test and evaluate things with an open mind and avoid a critical spirit.

Over the years, I have seen many leaders miss something God was trying to do for them because they could not be open enough to evaluate or test something without a predetermined bias. Ask yourself, "How am I responding to other followers of God who have different experiences than I do?" "When is the last time God did something outside of my box or my paradigm and I was open enough to recognize God and learn something new?" "Am I open enough to God to let him expand my paradigms and experiences?"

Abram

Every time I go through the story of Abram, I am astounded at his responses to God. So much could be written about Abram's journey with God. He did not always get it right, but his openness to God, his willingness to learn, and his ability to grow in his faith is an incredible example for us. There are many lessons to learn from Abram, but I just want to focus on one thing here.

How did Abram know that it was God speaking to him? In Genesis 12, God asked Abram to leave his country, his culture, his people, and his family to go to a place he had never been to. Abram demonstrated amazing openness just to be willing to listen to God, let alone act on what he heard. The fact that he does makes the story almost unbelievable. After all, he did not have any traditions to follow. There were no best-selling books with God stories to help Abram discern God's voice. He did not have history books outlining the interactions between God and people. He did not have a community of people that he could ask to help him discern if the voice inside his head was God or not. How did he know it was God?

The "voice of God" told him to leave and go. In his hometown, there were hundreds of different temples and gods to choose from. Out of this cultural setting, how did Abram know God? I do not think Abram could have known. He chose to believe. His openness to trust God for the journey of faith is the most amazing thing about the story. As Abram journeyed with God and wrestled with his faith, God revealed more and more about himself and his faithfulness. We can benefit from Abram's story because we can learn so much about the God "Yahweh" and about how to respond in faith. Abram's initial response to the call of God in the midst of uncertainty and insecurity says to me, "Be ready." Our own responses in faith will more than likely involve a lot of uncertainty and insecurity. These vulnerabilities test our faith and our openness to God. I am so grateful that we have the story of Abram to learn from. It challenges me to consider my own faith and openness, "Am I open to God? Am I open to hearing God say something to me like 'leave and go'?"

Martha

I think Martha gets a bad rap sometimes. Most of the time she is spoken about, she is used as an example of what we should not be like. I think this is unfortunate because she demonstrated a kind of spiritual hunger and faith that few people around Jesus did. In John 11, her brother Lazarus got sick. In this crisis, Martha and her sister Mary moved into action. They sent immediately for their friend Jesus. They go through great disappointment and pain at the death of their brother. Jesus was delayed for four days before he finally responds. Martha heard that Jesus was coming and runs to him. There was an immediate response inside of her to Jesus while her sister Mary stayed at home.

Do you realize that Martha was the person who experienced one of the deepest expressions of emotion, love, and power that came from Jesus during his earthly ministry? It was to Martha that Jesus reveals, "I am the resurrection and life." He was talking to Martha as they went to the tomb of Lazarus. She was standing right beside him when the tomb was opened. We know this because she was the one who made the comment about the smell of the decomposing body that had been in the tomb for four days.

She was a first hand witness of the resurrection of Lazarus! How do you think the words of Jesus about resurrection and life came alive in her while she was standing there? What do you think this did to her faith and her relationship to Jesus? I would love to have the kind of spiritual hunger and faith that Martha had. God responds to that kind of person. She does the one thing that every person should do in the midst of great pain, she let her pain drive her to Jesus. There are a lot of painful moments that we as leaders will face in life. Martha would whisper in our ear, "Send for Jesus and when he comes, run to him. When Jesus is present, we can expect a touch of resurrection and life."

Nicodemus

What do you think about when you hear the name Nicodemus? I think about one thing: He really wanted to learn. His willingness to learn pushed him past a number of significant barriers to get to Jesus. In John 3, he approached Jesus after dark and experienced a profound spiritual encounter. Most of us know the incredible things Jesus said in chapter 3, but do we remember that Jesus was talking to Nicodemus?

What do you think happened to Nicodemus as a result of this talk? Did Nicodemus experience a touch from God? Did his conversation with Jesus change him? I think so. He is mentioned twice more in the gospel of John. In John 7, during an interaction when Jesus was being attacked and rejected by his fellow religious leaders, we are told that Nicodemus spoke up in defense of Jesus. He is not in the shadows any longer. He went on public record with his support of Jesus.

Then in John 19:38-42, after Jesus was crucified, Joseph of Arimathea asked for the body of Jesus. It was Nicodemus who accompanied him and it was Nicodemus who brought the expensive burial cloth and perfumes to wrap Jesus in. I think that these two passages show the profound effect that Jesus had on him. When Jesus rose from the dead and came out of the tomb to meet with his followers, do you think Nicodemus was there? We do not know, but I imagine that he was one of the 500 that Jesus appeared to (I Corinthians 15). He may have even been in the upper room with the Apostles praying and waiting for the promised coming of the Holy Spirit (Acts 1). His openness and willingness to learn is worth emulating. That hunger for truth will always lead us to an encounter with Jesus himself.

Jeremiah

How will we respond to rejection? How will we respond to the lack of success? How will we respond to setbacks? Every leader will face these questions. There is no way around them. If we stay in ministry, we will have to deal with them.

Have you read through Jeremiah's call to ministry lately? God said, "Get yourself ready. Stand up and say whatever I tell you. Don't be afraid or I myself will pour out fear on you in front of your enemies. You will stand and speak against everyone and everything. They will fight against you but they will not overcome you for I am with you and I will rescue you" (Jeremiah 1:17-19, NIV).

Could you imagine being called to a lifetime ministry of rejection and fruitlessness? How did Jeremiah do it? I bet there are some of us that can relate to some of Jeremiah's experiences. Maybe we cannot relate to a lifetime of this kind of rejection from people, but we can relate to feeling afraid. We can relate to feeling as though we are not gifted enough or not feeling ready for what God has asked us to do. We can relate to a sense of fruitlessness or to being criticized and rejected.

In today's vernacular, we talk about being led "into the desert." Rejection, criticism, fear, and a sense of inadequacy will lead us into the desert. It is a place that most leaders become familiar with sooner or later. It is a place where many leaders encounter their true self. It is a place of testing, *but it is also the place where we encounter the living God. It can be a place of renewal.*

Jeremiah's story is an amazing story about strength. How did Jeremiah get the strength he needed to keep going? What renewed Jeremiah? How did he find energy to keep going? Jeremiah answers to these questions as he described his interactions with God in the midst of his own desert experiences.

There are six times where Jeremiah cries out to God and complains. Each time, Jeremiah was suffering and he turned to God. Each time, Jeremiah was reminded of the promise that God made to him when He called Jeremiah to his prophetic ministry. God pointed him back to the beginning and reminded Jeremiah what he promised him. God reminded Jeremiah that he was with him and would rescue him.

Jeremiah turned into God in the really difficult times. He kept going back to God and addressed his complaints directly to him. He did not go somewhere else or to someone else to complain. I know that when I have gone through really difficult times, I like to tell other people about it. Sometimes it is hard for me to go to God because he is the one I am disappointed with or frustrated about. God is not doing what I want him to do, but I do not want to say it directly to him. Jeremiah's example is so valuable for us. God can handle it when we bring our tough stuff to him. I love God's response to Jeremiah, he reminded him of the promises that he made to him.

This whole story reminds me to ask myself a few important questions on a regular basis. "Where do I go when I am complaining?" "When I am really hurt, rejected, unmotivated, frustrated, and tempted to quit, where do I turn?" "What promises has God made to me that I am standing on?" If I turn into God, I know he will be with me and respond according to his purposes in his timing!

Journey Well

Have you ever gone on a long journey in the car? In the last few years, we have taken about five long trips in the car. There is one trip that we have taken twice. We have driven from our home in Colorado to visit my family in California. That trip reminds me a lot of the journey through life and leadership development. We start out with an excitement and enthusiasm and there is a lot of interesting scenery in the first part of the trip. Then comes a long section of relatively monotonous desert like scenery in the middle. After that comes the awareness that we are nearing California and the excitement of reaching our family at the end of the journey as we pulled into my parent's driveway. The beginning and the end have different dynamics than the middle. Getting started carries a certain kind of excitement. Finishing and arriving are also rewarding. The long stretch in the middle does not have a lot that makes it exciting. Faithfully, consistently, carefully and persistently continuing along the road is what the middle is all about.

In this book, we have described the middle section of the journey as leaders. We have described a lot of issues that leaders may have to face and challenges that they have to overcome. The middle part of the journey may not be as exciting as the beginning. We continue to deal with the issues that we discovered in our foundations. We continue to grow into maturity as we attend to the strengthening of our foundation. And we have to avoid the pitfalls and traps along the way. It is a period of faithfulness, learning to be consistent, persevering, growing, taking on more responsibility, and maturing in who we are and what we are to do. It is the longest phase of our leadership development and will determine whether we finish well and leave a lasting legacy.

As I shared earlier in this chapter, being open to God is absolutely critical if we are going to make it through the middle part of the journey. Our openness to God is directly related to our attitude concerning our willingness to learn. When we are open to God, he will meet us and make sure that we have what we need in the middle of our journey. This can infuse a whole new level of interest and build some excitement into the middle stages. What is most important to remember about the journey is that God is committed to helping us reach our destination and he is committed to being with us on the journey.

So... journey well!

Evaluation and Application

1. What did you learn about openness from I Corinthians 10? Why is openness especially important for leaders as they attempt to navigate mid-life challenges?

2. What did you learn about hospitality and the lordship of Christ from John 1? What are the issues in your life that keep you from allowing Christ to take complete residency in your life?

3. Which of the Biblical examples (King Saul, Zechariah, the Religious Leaders and Jesus, Abram, Martha, Nicodemus, or Jeremiah) did you most identify with? Why and what insights did you gain?

4. What do you need to do to make sure that your spiritual foundation is strong enough to navigate mid-life and prepare you to finish well and leave a lasting legacy?

Appendix A

Love Inventory

"Love is patient, love is kind. It does not envy, it does not boast, it is not proud. It is not rude, it is not self-seeking, it is not easily angered, it keeps no record of wrongs. Love does not delight in evil but rejoices with truth. It always protects, always trusts, always hopes, always perseveres. Love never fails." I Corinthians 13: 4-8 (NIV)

- Patient (*makrothumia*) – "long suffering"

- Kind (*chrestotes*) – "goodness of heart, serviceable, pleasant"

- Does not envy (*zeloo*) – "indignation, jealousy [to have what others have]"
- Does not boast (*perpereuomai*) – "to vaunt oneself, vainglory, brag"
- Is not proud (*phusioo*) – "to puff up, blow up, inflate [with pride]"
- Is not rude (*aschnmomai*) – "to act unbecomingly [at the expense of others]"
- Is not self-seeking (*zeteo*) – "to strive after, endeavor, desire [self]"
- Is not easily angered (*orge*) – "gradual, long lasting anger"
- Does not keep a record of wrongs (*kakos*) –"injurious, destructive [hurtful]"
- Does not delight in evil (*adikeo*) – "unrighteousness, to do wrong"
- Rejoices with truth (*alethes*) – "real, ideal, genuine"
- Always protects (*stego*) – "to cover, conceal, ward off, resist"
- Always trusts (*pisteuo*) – "to entrust, to commit to one's trust"
- Always hopes (*elpizo*) – "favorable and confident expectation, happy anticipation of good"
- Always perseveres (*hupomeno*) – "to bear up courageously [under suffering]"

- Never fails (*pipto*) – "to fall, loose authority, or cease to have force [sufficient for the need]"

Self-Evaluation: Please circle the number that best represents your practice of the following characteristics of love.

1– weak 2- inconsistent 3- average 4- consistent 5- strong

Characteristic:	Rating:				
1. Patient ("long suffering")	1	2	3	4	5
2. Kind ("goodness of heart, serviceable, pleasant")	1	2	3	4	5
3. Does not envy ("indignation, jealousy [to have what others have]")	1	2	3	4	5
4. Does not boast ("to vaunt oneself, vainglory, brag")	1	2	3	4	5
5. Is not proud ("to puff up, blow up, inflate [with pride]")	1	2	3	4	5
6. Is not rude ("to act unbecomingly [at the expense of others]")	1	2	3	4	5
7. Is not self-seeking ("to strive after, endeavor, desire [self]")	1	2	3	4	5
8. Is not easily angered ("gradual, long lasting anger")	1	2	3	4	5
9. Does not keep a record of wrongs ("injurious, destructive [hurtful]")	1	2	3	4	5
10. Does not delight in evil ("unrighteousness, to do wrong")	1	2	3	4	5
11. Rejoices with truth ("real, ideal, genuine")	1	2	3	4	5
12. Always protects ("to cover, conceal, ward off, resist")	1	2	3	4	5
13. Always trusts ("to entrust, to commit to one's trust")	1	2	3	4	5

14. Always hopes 1 2 3 4 5
("favorable and confident expectation, happy anticipation of good")
15. Always perseveres 1 2 3 4 5
("to bear up courageously [under suffering]")
16. Never fails 1 2 3 4 5
("to fall, loose authority, or cease to have force [sufficient for the need]")

Appendix B

Burnout Inventory

Prayerfully read through the following list of warning signs of burnout and circle any of them that you sense you are weak or vulnerable in.

1. Inconsistent devotional life (loss of sense of presence and peace of God).

2. Inability to manage daily schedule (regularly working more than 8 hour days).

3. Inconsistent day off (at least once per week).

4. Lack of recreational interests and regular exercise (2-3 times per week).

5. Frequent fatigue, discouragement, or depression (prone to sickness).

6. Lack of enjoyment in life and ministry (frequent thoughts of quitting).

7. Frequent friction with spouse and children (easily frustrated and angry).

8. Frequent friction with boss and staff or co-workers (easily impatient and judgmental).

9. Growing number of uncompleted tasks, projects (missed appointments and unfulfilled commitments).

10. Disconnection relationally with mentor(s) (lack of accountability).

Add up the number of statements that you circled and see what range you are in:

0-2 OK, make sure that you are guarding and maintaining your intimacy with God.

3-6 DANGER, evaluate honestly and take remedial action necessary to regain intimacy with God.

7-10 CRISIS, stop what you are doing ASAP, get help, and take whatever remedial action necessary to regain intimacy with God.

Appendix C

Blowout Inventory

Prayerfully read through the following list of warning signs of blowout and circle any of them that you sense you are weak or vulnerable in.

1. Secret life involving fantasy or behavior (eventually leading to bondage).

2. Justification of behaviors as personal "rights or liberties" (at the expense of living a life above reproach).

3. Inconsistent devotional life (loss of sense of presence and peace of God).

4. Lack of accountability (unwilling to be teachable and surrounding yourself with "yes" people).

5. Insistence of having your own way (dogmatic, argumentative, unwilling to compromise on "non-essentials").

6. Pragmatic approach to life and ministry (the end justifies the means).

7. Blaming circumstances or others for problems (which can come from a root of bitterness).

8. Tendency to use people up rather than build them up (viewing people as means rather than the end of ministry).

9. Neglect of primary relationships (spouse, children, key leaders or staff).

10. Dependence on personal power rather than spiritual authority (flesh versus spiritual power).

Add up the number of statements that you circled and see what range you are in:

- 0-2 OK, make sure that you are guarding and maintaining your integrity with God.
- 3-6 DANGER, evaluate honestly and take remedial action necessary to regain integrity with God.
- 7-10 CRISIS, stop what you are doing ASAP, get help, and take whatever remedial action necessary to regain integrity with God.

Appendix D

Plateauing Inventory

Prayerfully read through the following list of warning signs of plateauing and circle any of them that you sense you are weak or vulnerable in.

1. A series of failures leading to a lack of confidence (in God) leading to self-preservation; or a series of success leading to self-confidence and self-promotion.

2. Confusion and frustration about God's will and an eventual loss of assurance in God's calling and purpose in life and ministry.

3. Loss of idealism and passion for something better and a default to maintenance and keeping the peace.

4. Looking to something outside of your current situation for fulfillment (i.e. another position, a promotion, etc.).

5. A growing apatite for materialism and creature comforts as a basis of worth and security (whether you have money or not).

6. A growing unwillingness to make the hard decisions (laissez-faire approach) or making the hard decisions without due process (authoritarian approach).

7. Covering your backside, taking care of your own needs first and foremost, and becoming more and more cynical.

8. Becoming more critical or passive-aggressive of other's creative, change oriented ideas, especially if they mean change, loss of control or influence, or more work for you.

9. Holding on to current positions, even if you are unfulfilled and unfruitful, because you do not know what to do next or are afraid of the uncertainty of stepping out in faith.

10. Growing tendency to Isolate oneself from people of faith and hang with the veterans of the organization that are hanging on until retirement.

Add up the number of statements that you circled and see what range you are in:

- 0-2 OK, make sure that you are guarding and maintaining your trust in God.
- 3-6 DANGER, evaluate honestly and take action necessary to regain trust in God.
- 7-10 CRISIS, stop what you are doing ASAP, get help, and take whatever remedial action necessary to regain trust God.

Appendix E

Accountability Inventory (adapted from Linda Galindo, ***The 85% Solution***, "Your Personal Accountability Quotient", p. 225-231)

Rank yourself on the following questions/statements using the following scale:

1. I currently have spiritual mentors in my life:

1 2 3 4 5

2. I meet at least once per month with a spiritual mentor:
1 2 3 4 5

3. I am accountable for the action plans I commit to:
1 2 3 4 5

4. I don't make excuses or blame when I don't meet my goals:
1 2 3 4 5

5. I am open to constructive criticism from my mentor:
1 2 3 4 5

6. I seek advice from my mentors before making difficult decisions:
1 2 3 4 5

7. I am accountable for results even in difficult circumstances:
1 2 3 4 5

8. I am interested in personal growth:
1 2 3 4 5

9. I am interested in developing my leadership potential:
1 2 3 4 5

10. I am a life-long learner:
1 2 3 4 5

Add up your total points (somewhere between 10 and 50) and use the following scale to asses you accountability level. Scale:

10-20 Healthy Accountability
21-35 Limited Accountability
36-50 Vulnerable

Resources

the Convergence group (theconvergencegroup.org)

Leadership Development Series by Paul Leavenworth

The Discipleship and Mentoring Workbook
The Bible-Centered Leader Workbook
The Spirit-Empowered Leader Workbook

Finishing Well Series by Paul Leavenworth,

Finishing Well
Deep Processing
The Extraordinary Power of a Focused Life

Discovery Learning Resources by Paul Leavenworth

Small Group Facilitator Training (DVD)
Focused Life Workshop (DVD)
Finishing Well (DVD)

Coaching

Focused Life Workshop (with 4 follow-up coaching appointments)
Focused Life 1 On 1
L/Bt Coach Certification (with Terry Walling)

The Clinton Institute (jtclintoninstitute.com)

Leadership Books by J. Robert Clinton

The Making of a Leader
Connecting (with Paul Stanley)

Well Series by Richard Clinton and Paul Leavenworth

Starting Well
Living and Leading Well
Finishing Well

Leader/Breakthru (leaderbreakthru.com)

Stuck! Series by Terry Walling

Stuck!
Awakening
Deciding
Finishing

Coaching

TRAC
ReFocusing
L/Bt Coach Certification

Bibliography

Bible Study Resources

The Contemporary Parallel New Testament, 1997, Oxford University Press

The International Standard Bible Encyclopedia, Geoffrey W. Bromiley (editor), 1979, Eerdmans Publishing

Elwell, Walter. Topical Analysis of the Bible, 1991, Baker Books

Vine, W.E. Vine's Complete Expository Dictionary of Old and New Testament Words, 1996, Nelson Publishers

Theology

Boice, James Montgomery. Foundations of the Christian Faith, 1986, InterVarsity Press

Driscoll, Mark and Gerry Breshears. Doctrine, 2010, Crossway

Duffield, Guy. Foundations of Pentecostal Theology, 1987, LIFE

Grudem, Wayne. Bible Doctrine, 1999, Zondervan Publishing

Packer, James. Knowing God, 1973, InterVarsity Press

Theology of the Holy Spirit

Green, Michael. I Believe in the Holy Spirit, 1985, Eerdmans
Lloyd-Jones, Martyn. Joy Unspeakable, 1984, Shaw Publishers
The Sovereign Spirit, 1985, Shaw Publishers
Wimber, John. Power Evangelism, 1986, Harper & Row
Power Healing, 1987, Harper & Row
Power Points, 1991, Harper & Row

Discipleship and Disciple-Making

Arnold, J. Heinrich. Discipleship, 1994, Plough Publishing House
Bailey, Keith. Care of Converts, 1997, Christian Publications
Barna, George. Growing True Disciples, 2000, Issachar Resources
Bonhoeffer, Dietrich. The Cost of Discipleship, 1995, Touchstone/ Simon and Schuster
Briscoe, Stuart. Discipleship for Ordinary People, 1995, Shaw Publishers
Cole, Neil. Cultivating a Life for God, 1999, ChurchSmart Resources
Coleman, Robert. The Master Plan of Discipleship, 1987, Revell Company
Cosgrove, Francis. Essentials of Discipleship, 1988, Roper Press
Drane, John. After McDonaldization, 2008, Baker Books
Eims, Leroy. The Lost Art of Disciple Making, 1978, Zondervan Press
Ferguson, Gordon. Discipling, 1997, Discipleship Publications
Finney, Charles. Principles of Discipleship, 1988, Bethany House Publishers
Grounds, Vernon. Radical Commitment, 1984, Multnomah Press
Hanks, Billie and William Shell (editors). Discipleship, 1981, Zondervan Press
Henrichsen, Walter. Disciples are Made not Born, 1988, Victor Books

Hull, Bill. Building High Commitment in a Low Commitment World, 1995, Revell Company
New Century Disciplemaking, 2001, Revell Company
Kincaid, Ron. A Celebration of Disciple-Making, 1990, SP Publications
Ortiz, Juan Carlos. Disciple, 1995, Charisma House
Petersen, Jim. Lifestyle Discipleship, 2007, NavPress
Rabey, Steve and Lois (editors). Side by Side, 2000, Cook communications
Robertson, Roy. The Timothy Principle, 1986, NavPress
Wallis, Arthur. The Radical Christian, 1981, Revell Company
Watson, David. Called and Committed, 1982, Shaw Publishers

Spiritual Formation

Blackaby, Henry & Claude King. Experiencing God, 1994, Broadman & Holman
Foster, Richard. Celebration of Discipline, 1998, Harper One
Kreider, Larry. Hearing God, 2005, House to House Publications
Lea, Larry. The Hearing Ear, 1988, Creation House
Smith, James Bryan. The Good and Beautiful God, 2009, InterVarsity Press
Stanley, Charles. How to Listen to God, 1985, Nelson Publishers
Tan, Siang-Yang and Douglas Gregg. Disciplines of the Holy Spirit, 1997, Zondervan Publishing
Virkler, Mark. Dialogue with God, 1986, Bridge Publishing
Whitney, Donald. Spiritual Disciplines for the Christian Life, 1991, NavPress
Willard, Dallas. The Spirit of the Disciplines, 1988, Harper & Row
Hearing God, 1999, InterVarsity Press
Willard, Dallas and Don Simpson. Revolution of Character, 2005, NavPress

Brokenness and Humility

John of the Cross (translated and edited by E. Allison Peers). Dark Night of the Soul, 1990, Image Books

Kelly, Thomas. A Testament of Devotion, 1941, Harper & Row Publishers

Murray, Andrew. Humility, 1982, Whitaker House

Nee, Watchman. The Breaking of the Outer Man and the Release of the Spirit, 1997, Living Streams Ministry

Nelson, Alan. Broken in the Right Places, 1994, Thomas Nelson Publishers Embracing Brokenness, 2002, NavPress

Nori, Don. The Power of Brokenness, 1997, Destiny Image Publishers

Nouwen, Henri. Turn My Mourning Into Dancing, 2001, Word Publishing

Stanley, Charles. The Blessing of Brokenness, 1997, Zondervan

Suffering and Trials

Damazio, Frank. From Barrenness to Fruitfulness, 1998, Regal

Davis, Ron Lee. Gold in the Making, 1983, Thomas Nelson Publishers

MacArthur, John. The Power of Suffering, 1995, Victor Books

Reccord, Bob. Forged by Fire, 2000, Broadman & Holman Publishers

Schaeffer, Edith. Affliction, 1993, Baker Books

Sorge, Bob. Pain, Perplexity and Promotion, 2002, Oasis House

Sproul, R. C. Surprised by Suffering, 1989, Tyndale House

Spurgeon, C. H. The Suffering of Man and the Sovereignty of God, 2001, Fox River Press

Stanley, Charles. How to Handle Adversity, 1989, Thomas Nelson Publishers

Church History

Cairns, Earle. Christianity Through the Centuries, 1982, Zondervan Publishing

Latourette, Kenneth Scott. A History of Christianity, Vol. I & II, 2005, Prince Press

Shelley, Bruce. Church History in Plain Language, 1995, Nelson Publishers

Biographies

Beeson, Ray and Ranalda Mack Hunsicker. The Hidden Price of Greatness, 1991, Tyndale

Edman, V. Raymond. They Found the Secret, 1984, Zondervan

Meyer, F. B. Classic Portraits Series (Abraham, David, Elijah, Israel, Jeremiah, John, Joseph, Joshua, Moses, Paul, Peter, Samuel), reprint 1990, Christian Literature Crusade

Rumph, Jane. Stories From the Front Lines, 1996, Chosen Books

Sciacca, Fran. Wounded Saints, 1992, Baker Books

Skoglund, Elizabeth. Wounded Heroes, 1992, Baker Books

Swindoll, Charles. Great Lives From God's Word Series (David, Esther, Elijah, Jesus, Job, Joseph, Moses, Paul), 1997-2008, Word Publishing

Whittaker, Colin. Seven Guides to Effective Prayer, 1987, Bethany House

Mentoring

Anderson, Keith and Randy Reese. Spiritual Mentoring, 1999, InterVarsity Press

Biehl, Bobb. Mentoring, 1996, Broadman and Holman Publishers

Boshers, Bo and Judson Poling. The Be With Factor, 2006, Zondervan Press

Bruce, A.B. The Training of the Twelve, 1971, Kregel Publications

Clinton, J. Robert and Paul Stanley. Connecting, 1992, NavPress

Coleman, Robert. The Master Plan of Evangelism, 2007, Revell Company

Creps, Earl. Reverse Mentoring, 2008, Jossey-Bass

Davis, Ron Lee. Mentoring, 1991, Nelson Publishers

Elliston, Edgar (editor). Teach Them Obedience in All Things, 1999, William Carey Library

Elmore, Tim. Mentoring, 1998, EQUIP

The Greatest Mentors in the Bible, 1996, Kingdom Publishing

Engstrom, Ted. The Making of a Mentor, 2005, World Vision

The Fine Art of Mentoring, 1989, Wolgemuth and Hyatt Publishers

Forman, Rowland, et al. The Leadership Baton, 2004, Zondervan Press

Jones, Laurie Beth. Jesus, Life Coach, 2004, Nelson Publishers

Harkavy, Daniel. Becoming a Coaching Leader, 2007, Nelson Publishers

Hendricks, Howard. As Iron Sharpens Iron, 1995, Moody Press

Standing Together, 1995, Vision House

Houston, James. The Mentored Life, 2002, NavPress

Krallmann, Gunter. Mentoring for Mission, 1992, GEM

Kreider, Larry. Authentic Spiritual Mentoring, 2008, Regal Books

The Cry for Spiritual Fathers and Mothers, 2007, House to House Publications

Luce, Ron (editor). Turning the Hearts of the Fathers, 1999, Albury Publishing

Ogden, Greg. Transforming Discipleship, 2003, InterVarsity Press

Otto, Donna. Finding a Mentor, Being a Mentor, 2001, Harvest House

Pue, Carson. Mentoring Leaders, 2005, Baker Books

Schultz, Steve and Chris Gaborit. Mentoring and Fathering, 1996, Christian International Ministries

Stoddard, David. The Heart of Mentoring, 2003, NavPress

Stoltzfus, Tony. Leadership Coaching, 2005, Coach22

Harvard Business Essentials: Coaching and Mentoring, 2004, Harvard Business School Publishing

Christian Leadership

Barna, George. The Power of Vision, 1992, Regal Books

Barna, George (editor). Leaders on Leadership, 1997, Regal Books

Blackaby, Henry and Richard Blackaby. Spiritual Leadership, 2001, Broadman and Holman Publishers

Blackaby, Henry and Kerry Skinner. Called and Accountable, 2002, New Hope Publishers

Clinton, J. Robert. The Making of a Leader, 1988, NavPress
Leadership Emergence Theory, 1989, Barnabas Resources
Clinton's Biblical Leadership Commentary, 1999, Barnabas Publishing

Clinton, Richard and Paul Leavenworth. Starting Well, 1994, Barnabas Publishing

Guinness, Os. The Call, 1998, Word Publishing

Hybels, Bill. Axiom, 2008, Zondervan

Malphurs, Aubrey. Being Leaders, 2003, Baker Books

Maxwell, John. Leadership Gold, 2008, Nelson Publishers

Sande, Ken. The Peacemaker, 2004, Baker Books

Sanders, J. Oswald. Spiritual Leadership, 1994, Moody Press

Stanley, Andy. Visioneering, 1999, Multnomah Publishers

Walling, Terry. Stuck! 2008, ChurchSmart

Marketplace Leadership

Bennis, Warren. On Becoming a Leader, 2003, Basic Books
Blanchard, Ken and Phil Hodges. Lead Like Jesus, 2005, Nelson
Burns, James MacGregor. Leadership, 1978, Harper & Row
Collins, Jim. Good to Great, 2001, Harper Business
Gardner, Howard. Leading Minds, 1996, Basic Books
George, Bill. True North, 2007, Jossey-Bass
Kouzes, Jim and Barry Posner. The Leadership Challenge, 2007, Jossey-Bass
Liu, Lan. Conversations on Leadership, 2010, Jossey-Bass
Pink, Daniel. Drive, 2009, Penguin Group
Szollose, Brad. Liquid Leadership, 2011, Greenleaf Books
Senge, Peter. The Fifth Discipline, 2006, Doubleday
Tichy, Noel. The Leadership Engine, 2005, Collins Business
Harvard Business Essentials: Manager's Toolkit, 2004, Harvard Business School Publishing